Wolf-Dieter Barz, Ingrid Kidder (Eds.)

The Sacra Infermeria Hospital of the Order of Malta at La Valletta

IUS VIVENS
Quellentexte zur Rechtsgeschichte

herausgegeben von

Prof. Dr. Heinz Holzhauer
Rechtswissenschaftliche Fakultät
(Universität Münster)

Dr. Wolf-Dieter Barz
Bundesverfassungsgericht Karlsruhe
(Bibliothek)

Prof. Dr. Andreas Roth
Institut für Rechtsgeschichte
(Johannes-Gutenberg-Universität Mainz)

Prof. Dr. Stefan Chr. Saar
Juristische Fakultät
(Universität Potsdam)

Band 9

LIT

Bibliographic information published by the Deutsche Nationalbibliothek
The Deutsche Nationalbibliothek lists this publication in the Deutsche Nationalbibliografie; detailed bibliographic data are available in the Internet at http://dnb.d-nb.de.

ISBN 978-3-643-90506-2

A catalogue record for this book is available from the British Library

©LIT VERLAG GmbH & Co. KG Wien,
Zweigniederlassung Zürich 2014
Klosbachstr. 107
CH-8032 Zürich
Tel. +41 (0) 44-251 75 05
Fax +41 (0) 44-251 75 06
E-Mail: zuerich@lit-verlag.ch
http://www.lit-verlag.ch

LIT VERLAG Dr. W. Hopf
Berlin 2014
Fresnostr. 2
D-48159 Münster
Tel. +49 (0) 2 51-62 03 20
Fax +49 (0) 2 51-23 19 72
E-Mail: lit@lit-verlag.de
http://www.lit-verlag.de

Distribution:

In the UK: Global Book Marketing, e-mail: mo@centralbooks.com
In North America: International Specialized Book Services, e-mail: orders@isbs.com
In Germany: LIT Verlag Fresnostr. 2, D-48159 Münster
Tel. +49 (0) 2 51-620 32 22, Fax +49 (0) 2 51-922 60 99, E-mail: vertrieb@lit-verlag.de

In Austria: Medienlogistik Pichler-ÖBZ, e-mail: mlo@medien-logistik.at
e-books are available at www.litwebshop.de

The Sacra Infermeria Hospital of the Order of Malta at La Valletta

Two legal sources

edited by
Wolf-Dieter Barz and Ingrid Kidder

Aber ein schöner Schmuck umgiebt Euch, die Schürze des Wärters,
Wenn Ihr, Löwen der Schlacht, Söhne des edelsten Stamm's,
Dienst an des Kranken Bett', dem Lechzenden Labung bereitet,
Und die niedrigste Pflicht christlicher Milde vollbringt.

Yet a beautiful ornament adorns you – the attendant's robe,
When you, lions of the battle, sons of the noblest breed,
Serve at the sick man's bed and quench the thirst of the parched man,
Fullfilling the lowly duty of Christian charity.

Friedrich von Schiller, from: Die Johanniter (1795)
Translation: *Albert Friggieri*

TABLE OF CONTENTS

Part I **9**

SPIRITUAL FOREWORD
(B. Kunhardt von Schmidt)..11

THE DEVELOPMENTS COVERING
THE SACRA INFERMERIA AT LA VALLETTA
(W.-D. Barz, I. Kidder)...17

SELECTIVE BIBLIOGRAPHY 45

FOOTNOTES 48

Part II..**57**

REGULATIONS OF THE HOSPITAL OF THE
KNIGHTS OF ST. JOHN AT VALLETTA
(W. K. R. Bedford) ....……………………………………….71

Part III...**159**

THE OLD AND NEW STATUTES OF THE ORDER
OF ST. JOHN OF JERUSALEM
(René Aubert [L'Abbe] de Vertot , ed.)………………………................162

Part I

SPIRITUAL FOREWORD

The sources discussed below open the doors to the history of the Order of Malta, also known as the Order of Saint John. They supplement the multiple publications which center on the oldest Christian order still in existence within the Western Patriarchate of Christendom.

Behind these doors lies the 900-year history of the Diaconate or Caritas, which took name and shape in a hall in Jerusalem for the poor, pilgrims, invalids and people in need of help. The name was borrowed from a small chapel near the church of Santa Maria Latina. The chapel was dedicated to John the Baptist, who is said to be the last prophet to have foresaid the appearance of God in the shape of Christ on Earth. The shape became manifested in a community considering itself as a grouping of disciples of Christ.

At the time, merchants who were deeply engaged in their faith in Christ took responsibility for their fellow human beings in a manner that Christ had commanded all Christians to observe. They considered themselves personally addressed by the word of Christ. Christ says, "When the Son of Man comes as King, and all the angels with him, he will sit on his royal throne, and all the earth's people will be gathered before him. Then he will divide them into groups, just as a shepherd separates the sheep from the goats: he will put the sheep at his right and goats at his left. Then the King will say to the people on his right, you that are blessed by my Father: come! Come and receive the Kingdom which has been prepared for you ever since the creation of the world. I was hungry and you fed me, thirsty and you gave me drink; I was a stranger and you received me in your homes, naked and you clothed me; I was sick and you took care for me, in prison and you visited me." (The Gospel of Sant Matthew 25:31-36, The New Testament in Today's English Version, 3rd edition, Days Inn, American Bible Society

1966,1971). Here, Jesus from Nazzareth enumerates the proverbial six acts of compassion, namely "feeding the hungry, giving drink to the thirsty, clothing the naked, receiving the strangers in your home, taking care of the sick and visiting the imprisoned, supplemented by the obligation to bury the dead" (cf. Rödel, p. 4). Only several years later was this community converted into a chivalric order under the supervision of one Brother Gerhard (cf. Rödel, p. 6). He also permitted crusaders to join the lay-brotherhood that originally did "not have the character of an order" (cf. Rödel, p. 6). In the beginning (between 1048 and 1071) they called themselves the Knights Hospitaller of the Chapel of Saint John in Jerusalem (cf. Rödel, p. 5). These men from the maritime Republic of Amalfi considered the service to humans in need of help, "the poor as one's masters", to be their life-work according to the six acts of compassion. "The treatment of the poor as one's masters originated in the comprehensive mandate of Jesus, "whenever you did this for one of the least important of these brothers of mine, you did it for me!" (The Gospel of Saint Matthew 25:40, The New Testament). There is strong evidence that the brotherhood under Brother Gerhard was promoted to a knightly order in 1099 (cf. Rödel, p. 6). A few years later this order, which was confirmed by Pope Pachalis II in 1113, had come to oversee an "institution" (Wolf-Dieter Barz, see below) for as many as 2,000 persons. Very soon it branched out and established other locations, notably hospitals, in other parts of the world.

The Order of Malta and its independent reformatory branch, the Bailiwick of Brandenburg of the Order of Saint John, is an exceptional phenomenon. Its beginnings do not lie in the usual course of time and power, the search for possessions, the explosion of knowledge, natural events of human plotting. In my opinion its origins are solely religious in nature (cf. v. Kaehne, 2nd paragraph).

Medieval society was dominated by religious debates and infighting. Salvation and the question of the Last Judgment were at the center of all human thought. Over many centuries Christ has spoken directly to man concerning what were, at the time, eminently important concerns, as proven by the verses 25 and 31-32a in the Gospel of Saint Matthew. The question of eternal life was a legacy of Antiquity.

The history of the origins of Islam also shows us that religious issues dominated everyday conversations and debates. During his rides through the desert, which frequently lasted for several weeks, Mohammed, travelling with merchant caravans, became the prophet Mohammed, a duty to which he considered himself called by the Archangel Gabriel. These caravans were also a melting pot for the world's religions.

So it is only natural to find that the Order of Malta's (Order of Saint John's) mission, as defined in the Order's initial charter, is based on the instructions of Jesus to his disciples, which Saint Paul later adapted and taught. Elsewhere, Saint Paul defines the main idea of Christian ethics and morals as follows: "For when we are in union with Christ Jesus ... all what matters is faith that works through love" (quoted from the Letter of Saint Paul to the Galatians 5:6. The New Testament in Today's English Version, see above). Love shows itself in the deeds of man and is reflected directly in the service we provide to our fellow human beings.

The Order's charter shows that charitable services to the poor as ordered by Christ were given without regard to person, race, gender or religious belief from the very beginning, since Christ was considered to be manifest in those whom they served. To this day, in the eyes of the Order's members the poor are still considered to be "our lords, the sick." To serve them means to serve Jesus Christ. The poor are closest to the Lord and are the first to be given a favorable hearing by Him. In this context Rödel alludes to the fact that the eight-pointed cross of the Order was originally a simple bar cross that the patron saint of the Order, John the Baptist, gave to his vassal the Order of Saint John as a coat of arms. Only later was it changed to the eight-pointed cross symbolizing Christ the Savior (6th-7th century AD), thereby acquiring its modern interpretation as the symbol of the eight Beatitudes (see Christ's Sermon on the Mount) (Rödel, p. 7). So the cross remains the same Cross as the one, on which Jesus died for the sins of all human beings.

Section XVIII of the Hospital charter of Roger de Molin dated 14 March 1181 (translated into German by v. Kaehne) reads, "And that the hospital brothers day and night serve the sick willingly as though they were their lords."

Following in the footsteps of the Lord Jesus Christ is the motivation behind all Christian charity. Until modern times it was carried by the desire, having been forgiven for all sins, to be seen by God as Jesus on the Cross and accepted into Heaven. Men wanted to be among the chosen few who would be allowed to follow Christ into resurrection from the dead. Today this motif has faded. Modern man prays less for "eternal salvation" than for mericiful dying and death. Salvation is only the secondary concern. Thanks to the Reformation and especially to the development of the Humanities during the Enlightenment (e.g. E. Kant's categorical imperative) humans can live with more self-confidence and are more at liberty to take their own decisions than was possible during Antiquity or in the Middle Ages.

Consequently, active charity has become more and more centered around nursing the sick as a necessary and identifiable commandment. Today, other manifestations of poverty are more or less taken care of by public-sector agencies (cf. Rödel, p. 14 ff.) The Order's modern-day activities reflect this change. The spiritual backdrop to the Christian mission that was embedded in Antiquity's concept of the *xenodochium* (a shelter or hostel for strangers) (cf. G. Rödel, p.5.) appears to have been narrowed. The sources make reference to the Order's original philosophy, namely that spiritual redemption, not the physical wellbeing of those who were received at the hospitals, was more important, v. Kaehne cites the oldest existing chapter of the Order, which dates back to 1125 and refers to the admittance of the sick to a hospital: "When a sick person comes into the house... he should be admitted in the following way: firstly he should confess to the priest, then receive communion and then he should be brought to bed, and here be fed as a lord according to the possibilities of the house before the brothers cat. On all Sundays the epistle and the gospel should be read in the house" (cf. v. Kaehne, p. 2).

The original mission of the Order of Malta (Saint John) is reflected in its charter, in its rules concerning the construction of the hospitals, their organizational structure, the care given to all residents (travellers, pilgrims, refugees, the poor, children, widows and orphans, and the sick), and the pastoral care given there. All of them should meet Christ the Lord through the service of the (Knights) Brethren of the Order. His words and actions should be revealed through them. Accordingly, it is my sincere wish that the presented research works may illuminate the mandate of the Order, which is to preach the joyful tidings of Jesus Christ.

Bernd Kunhardt von Schmidt

Translation by *Ulla Kunhardt von Schmidt*

THE DEVELOPMENTS COVERING
THE SACRA INFERMERIA AT LA VALLETTA

..... Yet a more beautiful ornament adorns you – the attendant's robe, when you, lions of the battle, sons of the noblest breed, serve at the sick man's bed and quench the thirst of the parched man, fulfilling the lowly duty of Christian charity .....
It was Friedrich von Schiller who wrote these lines of an epigram into the guest book of the Order. In his literary oeuvres he had dealt four times with the Order of St. John respectively the Order of Malta, as it was called later[1].

It is customary to consider this Order as the one of the Crusaders-Orders of the Knights of the Cross. Even as late as 1739 the well-known ZEDLER Encyclopaedia listed under

Malteser-Ritter (Knights of Malta):
Die Malteser-Ritter sind heutigen Tages die berühmtesten Ritter der Welt, welche sich sonderlich durch die Dienste, die sie der Christenheit wider die Ungläubigen geleistet, so berühmt gemacht ... - In our times the Knights of Malta are worldwide the most famous knights. Their great fame is based especially on the multiple services they rendered in their devotion to Christianity against the Infidels....[2].

Yet, it should be remembered that the origin of the Order is to be found in a hospital; the original, rather archetype of the community, was a hospitaller fraternity. Regarded from a theological viewpoint one might even say that the course of development of the Order from a Hospice or Hospitaller Order to a Crusader Order with mighty temporal powers had been a disastrous development for the Order of Malta. Also some words by Pope Alexander III

(1159-1181) may certainly be considered in this context: he reminded the Knights of the Order of the rules of their community namely to show more engagement in the assistance of the poor and the work of charity. Consequently they should refrain from combating with martial weapons – unless the banner of the Holy Cross was unfurled and the Kingdom of Jerusalem had to be defended or a hostile town to be conquered[3].

The aim of the present source edition is, however, not the military aspect of the Order, but prominence shall be given to the origin of the Order, its hospitals which were erected at every place the Order had to settle during the course of its turbulent and eventful history. The project at hand will deal with the *Sacra Infermeria* on Malta during the seventeenth and eighteenth century. This introduction does not deal with any specific detail of the *Sacra Infermeria*, on the contrary the reader is invited to visualize the Maltese Hospital by utilising these sources to enable him to form his own opinion. For the purpose of deepening this impression some references regarding the literature of the general history of the Order of Malta may be considered, as well as literature regarding the legal history concerning the Order, and relating to its hospital in La Valletta; and finally also the footnotes to this introduction may be of assistance.

In order to achieve a better understanding of this introduction a short sketch of the history of the Order is presented herewith:
Article 1) of the current Constitution of the Order names the confraternity as follows: *Sovrano Militare Ordine Ospedaliero di San Giovanni di Gerusalemme, detto di Rodi, detto di Malta.* Therewith title Article 1) renders a statement about the foundation and history of the Order. Initially the abridged version of the name was *Order of St. John* or *Hospitaller Order.* Only later and in fact still today the Order is called *Order of Malta* thus referring to its temporary headquarters on Malta. In this essay – irrespective of historical ref-

erences - the name used is often in form of an abbreviation: SMOM (*Sovrano Militare Ordine di Malta*).

The Order emerged from a congregation managing a hospice or hospital which was founded in Jerusalem about 1048 by some merchants in this historically very eventful and important area. St. John the Baptist was made the patron. Originally Charles the Great had ordered the erection of a *Muristan* on this same ground to serve as a hospital for the pilgrims to Jerusalem. Later, i.e. in 1046, this very site became the property of a merchant from the Sea-Trade Republic of Amalfi in Southern Italy. And this very community – men originating from Amalfi - developed into an Order in a canonical sense. Primarily their main objectives were the care and welfare of the pilgrims, and generally also of travellers, resulting gradually in a proper hospital undertaking.

Already in 1113 – meaning exactly 900 years ago - Pope Paschalis II recognises the community as an autonomous institution, mentions the hospitality in the Xenodochium, as well as satisfying the needs of the pilgrims and the poor[4]. Klement mentions in her book *Gottes Gastgeber, die Ritter des Hospitals von Jerusalem* (*Hosts of the Lord, the Knights of the Hospital at Jerusalem*) that in the beginning the Order's concern was applied quite generally to pilgrims and the poor. Only under Innozent II (1139-1143) emphasis was directed more to the *infirmi* or the *seignors malades*[5]. Showing respect and deference to its *guests* as well as supplying them with sufficient provisions was and still is a prominent part of the Order. Therefore and unlike the hospital of the Teutonic Order persons with a mental disorder were also accepted. In this respect the Hospitallers of St. John possibly followed the example of Arabian-Islamic hospitals. In their service at the hospitals they combined charity and love for God. Needy fellow human beings and deity – a similar combination of ideas was expressed by Cicero well before the Christian teachings would be of any influence:

Homines enim ad deos nulla re propius accedunt, quam salute hominibus dando. – In nothing men are more like Gods than in healing their fellow men (Oratio pro Q. Ligario, 38;1).

It may be assumed that in this way the Knights also took Jesus as a *Christus Medicus* to be an example. Although Jesus is not named as such in the New Testament, this title emerges during the times of early Christianity and could well have developed from the concepts of the periods of the Old Testament. (Wisdom of [Jesus ben] Sirach, Ecclus. 38:9, 10; Deut. 32:39; Exod. 15:26). It may be added that only fairly recently Woty Gollwitzer-Voll drew the attention to this ancient name of Christ and its signi-ficance[6].

St. Elizabeth - nearly at contemporary times – who after her demise would have liked to see her hospital in Marburg taken care of by the Order of Malta expanded this idea[7]. She demanded:

Seht, ich habe es Euch gesagt, wir müssen den Armen Freude bereiten. - Lo, I have told you, we must help the poor and please them.

The Knights of the Order of Malta were in fact not so far away from this idea. A few centuries later on Malta they tried to „please" the eyes of the patients with large paintings. Decorating the walls of the *Sacra Infermeria* by means of pictures meant the patients did not have to look at the plain walls of the rather dismal ward with those high and long walls. *(cf. "Of the Hangings and Pictures",* p. 93. It is surely not without reason one can find even today relevant hints, like for example by the Diocesan Council of Cologne for the caller service by priests mentioning the hand shake under the caption „How to make the patient happy."[8]

Relatively soon the Order of Malta took over the task of escorting its charges along the dangerous routes between Jerusalem and the Mediterranean ports of embarkation. These activities expanded to

such an extent that in time the SMOM became fully involved in the military activities within the states through which the crusaders passed. They even raised a regular army consisting of their own members. Consequently and from then on the now dominant *knight-monks* promised in addition to their usual vows to faithfully serve at the hospital as well as fight against the Islamic enemies.

This active service, as well as taking charge of the defence installations and even the responsibility over larger and nearly independent territories moulded the Order to an increasing extent into a military, chivalrous and nobiliary knightly Order of Crusaders, whereby a prominent tendency towards secularization prevailed. This politically important position certainly eased the way to establish a network of local and regional Order dependences also in Europe. However, during all these activities the Order never forgot to adhere to its hospitaller roots.

Due to the fact that the Order of Malta expanded also into a Military Order, the hospital of the Order developed as well into the special class of an early military hospital. It can be assumed that the Order's hospital was the first military hospital in the European cultural sphere since Roman Antiquity[9].

In 1291 SMOM and other Christian belligerent parties were forced to abandon the Holy Land. The Order took flight to Cyprus, and using this island as a base they conquered Rhodes and its neighbouring isles. The headquarters, i.e. the Convent, were transferred to the City of Rhodes in 1310. Very soon a hospital was erected, which is now in use by the *Archaeological Service of the Dodecanese*. Later on a spacious hospital with two floors was built near the Grandmaster's Palace. This building is presently used as a museum. By means of its naval force the Order served primarily as Christian naval police in the Aegean Sea. On New Year's Day of 1523 the Order had to give in once more to the Islamic Power – this time due to pressure exerted by the Turks, and abandoned its Order State on Rhodes.

SMOM - now based only on its naval fleet - roamed about the western parts of the Mediterranean for seven years until 1530. In this year Emperor Charles V, as King of Spain also ruling over the Kingdom of Sicily, invested the Order with a fief, namely Malta. To begin with the Order settled in the Maltese town of Birgu (Vittoriosa) and in the Fort of St. Angelo. Soon a new hospital was established in Birgu. And after the Order had valiantly beaten off a Turkish siege in 1565 and thus stopped the Turkish Mediterranean run on Europe, the new capital of Malta, i.e. La Valletta, was built. This city was erected on a narrow peninsular, and nearly at the point of this headland a new spacious hospital, the *Sacra Infermeria*, was constructed in several stages. Later – characteristically enough showing even more significance - this building was also called *Palazzo dello spedale*.

In his very recent reflections Michael Ellul maintains that the building was planned by the well-known Maltese architect Girolamo Cassar. This gentleman was also involved in the planning of La Valletta and was the mastermind of a number of layouts for buildings in this city as well as elsewhere on Malta[10]. Originally it was considered to erect Hospital and Convent Church – representing the two centres of the daily life of the Knight Monks - in close proximity. However, it was realized that the frequent chiming of bells would scarcely agree with the necessary peace the patients required for their recovery. Consequently a building site for St. John's Cathedral was chosen on a higher level of the peninsula, namely between the City Gate and the Grandmaster's Palace[11].

The Order allotted great importance to this undertaking which manifests itself in the extraordinary short building period. At the occasion of the Chapter General (legislative assembly of the Order) in

1574 the erection of the building was decided and already during the following year, i.e. after completion of the first building stage, the hospital started to accept patients It is assumed that the design of the building followed the Roman hospital *Santo Spirito* as an example. Eventually a capacity of about 740 in-patients was reached. If necessary, this number could be increased to 900, while other sources mention a figure as high as 2,000. However, according to yet a further source the beginning of erection is assumed to have taken place only in 1578, while the first construction stage was completed in 1582[12]. Also as far as the annual budget is concerned the hospital enjoyed voluminous ranking, for example its budget in 1788 was the highest after the amounts for the Order's naval and land forces.[13]

The knights accepted patients without any distinction regarding race, class or religious affiliation. Respective protests of the Inquisitor were simply disregarded by the Order[14]. Even slaves were accepted at the *Sacra Infermeria,* though in separate accommodations. The number of slaves in Malta fluctuated considerably, while there are 2,300 slaves recorded during the year 1664, a mere 1,000 are mentioned for 1749[15]. Generally the hospital was highly praised in Europe, and even additionally named *der Ruhm Maltas - the very glory of Malta*[16]. Today this old-time building has been refurbished to become a spacious modern Conference Centre.

The late Maltese *Chief Government Medical Officer* and Surgeon Attilio Critien expresses in his Preface to the book *Holy Infirmary Sketches* – while referring to the Hospital of the Order:

> ... that these „Sketches" may help one to get more intimately acquainted with one of the essential institutions of an Order whose presence here added considerably to the historical importance of our Islands ... [17].

The writer of the second preface *Justice William Harding* reminds the reader of the Maltese historian Albert Laferla, who *does not hesitate to state ... that, at that time, the Sacra Infermeria was the best hospital in the Mediterranean, if not in the whole of Europe*[18]. Freller speaks of *the most famous hospital of the Mediterranean at the time,* also of the *legendary reputation of the Sacra Infermeria*[19], and quotes elsewhere a manuscript from the archives of the Order from the sixteenth century[20]:

> Essendo l'Hospitalità, e la cure dell'Infermi il più principale, e primo obligo delli Religiosi di San Giovanni si trattiene ad imitatione di quella di Gerusalemme un'Infermeria molto bella nella città Valletta in Malta. – As hospitality and the care of the sick constitute the principal and primary duty of the professed (members of the Order) of Saint John [i.e. Knights of Malta] they maintain a very beautiful *Infermeria* on the model of that in Jerusalem in the city of Valletta in Malta.

In view of the quantity of various sources it is very astonishing that the medical historian Dieter Jetter in his book on European Hospitals acknowledges the *Sacra Infermeria* merely in two brief sentences[21].

In 1676 SMOM founded a medical Academy for Anatomy and Surgery, which later became the Medical Faculty of the University of Malta launched by the Order in 1771[22]. Thus the *Sacra Infermeria* became the first University Clinical Centre of Malta. Its speciality was that the corpses of hospital patients, as well as of all knights who had passed away, were dissected in order to support the anatomical lectures and studies.

Thomas Freller sums up the superior and exceptional significance of the Sacra Infermeria by considering the institution as a unique *Symbol and Raison d'être* of an entire state[23]. With reference to SMOM one could undoubtedly agree with Freller, considering that according to the ruling opinion the Order was already a subject of international public law independently of the Maltese territory, and was repeatedly named as *Ordensrepublik – a Republic of the Order* – as well as with other *termini technici* within the world of states[24]. Just as much as the medical charity presents the only purpose of the 'State' of the Order today, in former times charity also was - next to the anti-Islamic struggle - part of the purpose of the 'State'. However, the running of a hospital was entirely independent of the Order's territory, and the respective Statutes of the Order which prescribed a special purpose of the Order's 'State' were hardly part of the territorial constitution (of Malta). Though the Deed of Enfiefment of Emperor Charles V can certainly be apostrophized as the basic constitution of the Order State of Malta, this document points out another purpose of the territorial State:

> ..., and so that the Very Reverend and Venerable Grand Master, and our beloved sons .... should at length obtain a fixed Residence, and they should once more return to those duties for the benefit of Christendom which appertain their Religion; and should diligently exert their strength and their arms against the perfidious enemies of the Christian religion; ... [25].

Considering the strategic geographical interest prevailing at the occasion of the handing over of Malta to SMOM it is not very astonishing that merely the military dealings are listed as activities of the Order. The Deed of Enfiefment stipulates already a special purpose of the State of Malta: The island should serve the Order as a strategic basis for defence operations against the Islam. Therefore and seen from a constitutional view point the *Sacra Infermeria* could hardly have been the purpose of the State - the *Raison d'être* - of the Order State of Malta. However, the *Sacra Infermeria* had been an outstanding symbol of SMOM on Malta.

In 1798 Napoleon conquered Malta, and as a consequence SMOM had to vacate its Order State once more. Immediately with the arrival of Napoleon in 1798 the *Sacra Infermeria* became a military hospital – also later under the British rule, and was used as such until 1964. From then on the Order relocated a few times within in Europe – for some years even to St. Petersburg. Eventually the government of the Order moved to No. 68 Via Condotti in Rome. This building complex called PALAZZO MALTA had served originally as the Embassy of the Order in the Pontifical State. Accompanied by the privileges of the extraterritoriality the Grand Magistry is residing there to date still. Phenomenological one could now describe SMOM according to its constitution and international law as a state without territory – or in a play on words of Serra, *i.e.* as *Etat sans Etat*[26]. In recent times Reinhardt coined the equally fitting description *Personalstaat – State consisting of persons only*[27].

Just as in the early beginnings of its existence in Jerusalem the Order dedicates itself today to charity scopes only. But the Grand Magistry of the Order is not directly engaged in any individual hospital anymore.

Instead a well equipped ambulatory clinic has been established in the central main office building, offering services to citizens without means. This clinic has been refurbished and modernised recently, and in addition now also welcomes twice a week needy migrants lacking a residence permit. Especially these very needy people in their particular predicament would hardly be able to find or accept medical help in Rome without the assistance of this Order. In this context: these people benefit from the independent status of SMOM under international public law and its medical assistance. In other words: they are being treated beyond reach of Italian Sovereignty.

The *Grand Hospitaller* still ruling within the Order's hierarchy could be compared with a Minister of Health and supervises and coordinates central as well as decentralised medical activities of the entire *Maltese Order Family*. He pursues his work from Rome and is not the executive head of any hospital of the Order. In present times and in many parts of the world the hospitals or infermeria wards of the Maltese Order are operated according to the modern rather decentralised structures by the regional branches of the Order. Therefore these dependences are managed according to varying legal prevalences of the respective national law. Following the eight-pointed cross – which presumably can be attributed to the eight-pointed cross in the coat of arms of the Sea-Trade Republic of Amalfi - today approximately 13,500 members of the Order, a further 80,000 volunteers at the institutions of the Order and 25,000 employees in medical professions are serving in charity[28].

Omitted in this list are the members, volunteers etc. of the protestant, independent Order branches in Germany, in the Netherlands, Sweden and Great Britain. All these are exemplary in dedicating their endeavours in the same fields[29]. Mainly due to the changes the Reformation brought about, gradually protestant members of the Order could not participate in the development of the hospital on Malta anymore, especially as far as the erection of the *Sacra Infermeria* was concerned. And it is the *Sacra Infermeria* in La Valletta as well as all relevant and respective regulations which are dealt with primarily in this essay.

As far as the choice of time is concerned, it is mainly the eighteenth century which Alain Blondy in the subtitle of his book describes as *des dernières splendeurs à la ruine*[30]. This is a particularly dramatic chapter of the history of the Order, which basically still appears to be a continuum of a generally mediaeval ideology. It is only in modern times – similar to Phoenix rising from the ashes – for SMOM to take a step into present times by abandoning the by now anachronistic connections to the ideas of the crusader surroundings. One of the major reasons of this change was the newly re-developing emphasis and turn to hospital concepts or medical charity[31]. Without these changes there was a probability that the Order might have perished since leaving Malta. Its mere existence was often threatened since then.

Our brotherhood will be everlasting as the soil from which this flower grows is the poverty of the world and - with the help of God - there will always be people willing to reduce this poverty and make this misery bearable. (Epitaph of the beatified Gerhard, who is considered to have been the first Grandmaster of SMOM.)

This sentence of Gerhard, handed down by tradition and still often quoted, prognosticated then already that the original roots of the Order were destined to become a solid link into present times.

Though the eighteenth century still began for the Order with *splendeurs*, slowly symptoms of decline became perceptible to a degree that even outsiders could not help but noticing them. Neither did this development stop at the *Sacra Infermeria*. In 1725, however, the high quality awareness still existing in the administration of the Order's hospital emerges and shows itself once more in the phrasing of the source *Notizia della Sacra Infermeria* ... . The medical historian Edgar Erskine Hume comments as follows: *Like other famous establishments it* [the Order's hospital] *was subject to occasional criticism, but if the rules* [of the Notizia] *were obeyed, the good greatly outweighed the bad*[32]. As far as the legal recognition of the *Notizia* is concerned it is regrettable that the *theses ad licentiam in iure civile assequendam* („La vocazione ospedialiere di Cavalieri di S. Giovanni di Gerusalemme e d i Regolamenti della Sacra Infermeria di Malta, 1725") compiled 2001 by Antoniazzo Sterzi Barolo have never been published.

NOTIZIA
DELLA
SACRA INFERMERIA,
E
DELLA CARICA
DELLI COMMISSARJ
Delle Povere Inferme

IN ROMA.
Nella Stamperia di Rocco Bernabo, l'Anno del Giubileo MDCCXXV.
CON LICENZA DE' SUPERIORI.

REGOLAMENTO
DELLA
SACRA INFERMERIA
DI MALTA.

L Superiore, e Capo della Sacra Infermeria è l'EMINENTISSIMO, e REVEREN-DISSIMO GRAN MAESTRO, che s'intitola MAGNUS MAGISTER HOSPITALIS HIERUSALEM.

Il Grand' Ospidaliere Capo della lingua di Francia per sua antica preminenza presiede nell'Infermeria, al buon governo della quale invigila.

L'Infermiere è un Cavaliere Professo, al di cui zelo è raccomandata la Cura dell'Infermi, i quali deve provedere di letto, secondo la loro condizione, e bisogno; & abita nell' Infermeria in Appartamento separato. La mattina a buon'ora fa suonare la Visita, nella quale interviene per far' osservare con la dovuta carità dalli Medici l'Infermi, & acciò gli sia ordinato il bisognevole: Venuto poi il tempo del desinare fa suonare la Mangia per avisare tutti gl' Officiali, & assiste alla medesima acciò ogni letto abia la pitanza ordinatali, & ogn' uno de' Subalterni faccia il suo dovere; e lo stesso fa la sera nella Visita, e Cena. Deve sopra tutto far' osservare la dovuta quiete, e perciò di notte suol spesso visitare tutti i Letti, e Sale per la vigilanza delle Guardie, lumi, ed altro. E' sua ispezzione di far serrare alla solita ora di notte le porte, e portone dell' Infermeria, e procurare, che tutti gl'Officiali destinati siano riti-

Hume views the overall efficiency of the Order's hospital. However, what would have been the meaning or sense of the hospital achievements for the individual knight - for „*our Lords the Sick*"? As a matter of course the management of the hospital was executed by the members of the Order. It remains to be guessed which duties were carried out by the individual knight cloaked in *the attendant's robe ... fulfilling the lowly duty of Christian charity*? Which was the service the members of the Order really rendered as far as active charity help in the hospital was concerned? During most parts of the eighteenth century the Order consisted of seven active tongues, i.e. regional subdivisions of the Order, mostly developed or orientated by linguistic bounds. Consequently each tongue had to serve at the hospital for one day of the week. Concerning the specific activity on this particular weekday Joseph Camillieri reports: *The regulations published in that year* [1725] *make it very clear that the Knights' assistance of patients consisted only of the distribution of food*[33]. Thus it can be assumed that the hospitaller part of the Order restricted itself mainly to the support / maintenance and the management of the *Sacra Infermeria*. When Schiller – even in 1792 -writes about the lower service of the warden (meaning the knight) in the hospital, *who does not withhold himself from any of the disdainful services, from which our pampered senses would only turn way indignantly*[34], he has at least been mislead as far as the eighteenth century is concerned, or else he was visualising a totally different epoch of the Order.

Undoubtedly *Notizia* presents a very remarkable text – but what is the character behind it? Is *Notizia* a primary source, or a government document, or could it be that the text is authentic, yet more or less a „freely suspended" reflection, or could it possibly be a fake e.g. similar to the text of the Constitution of the Napoleonic Exile Princedom of Elba[35]. The text itself does not show any preamble or final clause which would identify the rules as legislative act of the respective authorities of SMOM. It is also evident that its structure does not follow the pattern of the extensive contemporary collections of statutes of the Order (see below page 41). For this reason and from a formal point of view, the text in itself does not hint towards any conclusion as far as its character is concerned.

Is the title page more predicative? The dominant element of the sheet is the Coat of Arms of the Order with coronet. Does the Coat of Arms – which after all is an official emblem – identify the text as „official"? One might remember, however, that the Coat of Arms decorates a great number of printed publications of the eighteenth century, whereby neither the author nor the contents are of official nature. Therefore the Coat of Arms is not a gauge of character of the *Notizia*[36]. In this context it may be mentioned Ballestrem having added, that the crown above the Coat of Arms represents the sovereignty of the Order[37]. Since the ruling time of Grandmaster Pinto (1741-1773) a hoop crown styled like a typical ducal crown decorated the Coat of Arms of the Order as well as the personal Coat of Arms of the Prince-Grandmaster[38]. In fact in early modern times the various forms of the closed crown indicated the sovereign status of their holders. Therefore the question arises whether the above mentioned open coronet is rather supposed to symbolise the principle of nobility of the Order of Malta.

On the title page Rome is stated as place of printing, which appears equally strange. In comparison, other works of the Maltese Order epoch were printed in the *Stamperia del Palazzo di Sua Altezza Ementissima* (i.e. Grandmaster's Palace) in La Valletta, likewise private prints as well as official printing matters, e.g. legal codification for the Order State Malta as well as for the Order itself[39]. However, the external place of printing is no special indication as regards the publishing year of 1725, reason being that between 1642 and 1756 very little was printed on Malta, instead printers on the Italian mainland were involved. It can be assumed that for prestige reasons the voluminous codifications of the Maltese Municipal

Law under Grandmaster Manoel de Vilhena indicate Malta as place of publication in 1724, although the Code of Law was in fact printed in Naples[40]. Therefore the fact of Rome being the actual place of printing does not speak against the officiality or the authenticity of the text of the *Notizia*.

What is the meaning of the addendum *con licenza de' Superiori*? The Maltese press laws were at least for certain times in so far quite impractical, as three independent authorities had to get into action. These were the Bishop, the Inquisitor and SMOM - each as autonomous censorship authority – they each had to pass the respective document to press. In Rome as the place of printing in the year 1725, however, circumstances were different. Therefore and due to the fact that the place of printing was Rome the papal censorship, and - because of Malta being country of origin - the Order's Council are to be assumed as authorities for the *Notizia* [41].

If according to the above the Order's Council had agreed to the printing, it could well be that it was indeed an official publication of the Order. Yet, and in any case, the Order had authorised the contents. Whether it would thus be an official printing matter can be left aside.

Verification whether the individual choice of words in any particular case could in fact be the reproduction of the original text, could possibly only be carried out if in the segment of the old Archives of the Order (today National Library), *Liber Conciliorum,* a relative document would exist which had been presented to the Order's Council as a manuscript[42]. As per today, this particular section of the archives has not been analyzed in detail; therefore special investigations would be required. However, in this context these would be rather superfluous, as even a warranted text shows adequately the course of a normal working day in the hospital.

In conclusion one should agree with the ungrounded statement of Ballestrem, i.e. that the *Notizia* represents one of the most important hospital rules of SMOM. Whether additionally they would present by-laws in the legal sense, listing finally the rules for caring of the „Poor Invalids" on Malta[43], is not a matter of consideration in this context.

The fact that the article has been printed at all manifests that the paper should have had a wide circulation and thus considered to be of importance. Could it be that the *Notizia* would have served the *Ospidalieri* as a „reminder of obligatory duties" especially for those members of the Order who according to their affiliation were not always assigned for service at the hospital? In any case due to the fact that universally there are only few copies available in public libraries a re-edition should be considered. It has to be noted that the *Notizia* is highly appreciated right from the beginning. After they had been presented to Pope Benedict XIII they were used as an example for some hospitals administered by the Holy See. This shows in a *breve* by the Pope, which was registered in the archives of La Valletta on 19th March, 1726. Also Zwehl, who had perused a vast amount of source material concerning the *Sacra Infermeria,* considered *Notizia* to be of such importance that he intended to add a certified copy to his oevre. This, however, never materialised[44].

Concerning the appreciation of the *Notizia*, the Order could well compare it with the times in Jerusalem. Dock and Stewart commented as follows: „At the height of its nursing excellence [in Jerusalem] the hospital regulations worked out by the Order of St. John were adopted by practically all the city hospitals or Maisons-Dieu as they arose in Europe. Its influence over mediaeval hospital management and nursing was therefore very great[45]. It is surprising that the Order's priest Antonio Micallef, who wrote about the statutes of the Order towards the end of the eighteenth century, and as

Professor also lectured about the same subject at *the University of Studies of Malta*, apparently did not enlarge on the rules for health and hospital matters and consequently did not mention the *Notizia* at all[46].

For the re-issuing of the *Notizia* it can be regarded as a lucky factor that William Kirkpatrick Riland Bedford, who published altogether three essays on SMOM [47] had already recognised this desideratum in the course of the nineteenth century. He published the *Notizia*, translated it into the English language, and incorporated it in the new edition. 33 years later Géraud Michel Comte de Pierredon published a French version of the *Notizia* [48]. Alas, also from Bedford's script are only few copies left. Even the National Library of Malta is not in possession of a copy, although Malta was a British Colony at the time of publishing. Therefore this particular script was chosen to be fully reproduced in the present publication (1882) under the title *The regulations of the old hospital of the knights of St. John at Valetta*. The translation of the *Notizia* by Hume - in the course of which he amends Bedford's version in several places – does by no means render a new edition of the work of Bedford superfluous. Reason being also that the much younger script by Hume has been located in German libraries only six times [49]. In addition Hume does not include the Italian version, and omits to include the paragraph *"Ecclesiastici"* instead saying only: „…which need not to be quoted here." [50]. Yet in saying so he does not do justice to the *Sacra Infermeria* as a hospital of an *Order*. Furthermore this way he disregards the transcendental purpose of a hospital and the longstanding views about illnesses, which obviously were also adhered to by the Order of Malta.

Since medieval times and finally until the Age of Enlightenment in the eighteenth century sickness was rather looked upon as God's punishment for misdemeanours [51]. During and after the Age of Enlightenment these ideas were processed and adapted in context with the – by now nearly forgotten - Pastoral Medicine. According to the prevailing belief it was not an urgent concern to 'meddle in God's business' by any therapeutic treatments, but instead primarily further the patient's reconciliation with God by means of spiritual care. Therefore one might say that hearing the confession at the moment of reception of a patient in the hospital was the first therapeutic step towards healing the patient's soul – and in doing so also his body. This may also be an explanation for the fact that the paragraph concerning the *Ecclesiastici* was placed before the *Delli Midici* in the *Notizia* under review. In every hospital ward - and as a matter of course - there was an altar for mass celebrations. From an architectural point of view this entity of caring for soul and sickness was best expressed in the erection of hospital churches. The nave was situated on the ground floor, and the hall above was dedicated to pilgrims, people in need, and the sick. These two halls were connected by means of openings in the vault above the areas important and used for the liturgy. This way it was possible for the people on the first floor to participate without any problem in all religious activities on the ground floor. The church of the Order Commandery in Niederweisel (Hesse) – today the spiritual centre of the Protestant Balley Brandenburg *(Johanniterorden)* – is an ideal shape and example of the hospital churches [52]. Apart from the general service acts at mass the hospital priests supported the patients individually especially with the sacraments, the confession, anointment of the sick (The Letter from Jacob 5:14-16), which would not be the last rites, as well as with the *Viaticum*.

The present source edition depicts a chronological counterpoint to the works of Lagleder and Klement, who dealt with the management of the Jerusalem hospital and issued its regulations [53]. Which coincidence might have led Bedford to the *Notizia*? In the *Oxford Dictionary of National Biography* the following is stated about Bedford: born 1826 in Sutton Coldfield, died 1905 in Circklewood, professions stated:

Antiquarian, Heraldist and Genealogist – in other words a person who was interested in history. Finally he studied theology, became *Rector* (vicar of an independent congregation) at his place of birth, member of a Freemason's Lodge, and he was a member of the regular clergy of *The most Venerable Order of the Hospital of Saint John of Jerusalem from 1778 to 1802* [54].

This particular branch of the Order had been founded in Great Britain and has strong tendencies towards Protestantism meaning Anglicanism. According to its homepage SMOM acknowledges this Order specifically as *Order of St. John* and does not consider it a *mimic order* [55].

It may have been a logical undertaking for Bedford to travel to the British Colony of Malta, to pay a visit to the former *Sacra Infermeria,* and to render a description of same in his introduction to the *Notizia.* According to his own account he discovered the *Notizia* in the archives in La Valletta. Anyhow, today it is registered in the Department for Archives of the *National Library*, under *AOM* (Archives of the Order of Malta) *No. 1713.* Originally this small book belonged to the stock of the Library of the Order Hospital. This Library was integrated into the Public Library – today the National Library – in 1776. The same fate was met by the manuscript *AOM No. 1714,* the *Regolamento per il governo spirituale, politico e economico del S. Ospedale dell' Ordine Gerosolimitano* (fols. I-VII, 215). According to Theresa Vann this contemporary manuscript is a transcript of the *Notizia* with annotations and subsequent changes of the rules placed on the left hand side of each page which had been left empty. This is followed by a copy of the rules of the year 1699, which had been enacted for medical doctors and surgeons during the rule of Grandmaster Raymond Perellos y Roccaful [56]. If Vann is right, it is astonishing that Bedford had never reported about this duplicate.

It is even more amazing, that Bedford, a theologian of the British branch of the Order, does not mention the religious background of the hospitaller engagement and thus neither the specific background of the hospital rules in his introduction. In order to address with this present source edition not only the legal and the medical historian but include also the view point of the third faculty namely *theology*, a pastor of the *Balley Brandenburg des Ritterlichen Ordens Sankt Johannis vom Spital zu Jerusalem (Johanniterorden)*, has commendably undertaken to bring up the religious importance of the hospital activities of the Order by his spiritual preface.

As already mentioned above, the eighteenth century was also the time of the decline and fall of the SMOM on Malta. Considering this, it could be regarded as Bedford's merits to have referred to this development in relevance to the *Sacra Infermeria* in the appendix. For this purpose he excerpts a report of the English philanthropist John Howard dealing with the social welfare institutions of SMOM on Malta, quoting from his book *An Account of the Principal Lazarettos in Europe*[57]. Howard gives prominence to the hospital traditions of the Order of Malta in reporting about the various institutions of the Order. Remembering that the hospital in the traditional sense of an all round „social ward" was the beginning, the origin of the Order as welfare centres. As preparation for this report Howard travelled extensively through a number of European countries including Malta during the year of 1786. This particular year is in so far significant as the reconnaissance trip of Howard fell into the period *before* the French Revolution. It is of vital importance to remember that during the Revolution the Order was stripped of all its assets situated in the then French areas. Consequently the Order also lost a considerable portion of its regular income. During the year 1795 this resulted even in melting down dispensable silver objects of the Sacra Infermeria in order to strike much needed coins. Therefore this significant loss which occurred in the budget cannot account for the grievances of the year 1786.

Other permanent budget impairments due to prevailing circumstances would hardly be as high as those due to the loss of income from France. Howard's *account* can be looked upon as an extremely reliable source. The much honoured author was so renowned for his work concerning research in prisons and hospitals that on the occasion of his demise in 1790 a number of *John Howard Halfpennies* were minted[58]. Recently Uwe Wesel in no less than four pages appreciated the philanthropist in his work *Geschichte des Rechts in Europa von den Griechen bis zum Vertrag von Lisbon - History of the Law in Europe from the period of the Greeks up to the Contract of Lisbon* [59].

In view of the present availability of sources an appropriate description of the *Sacra Infermeria* by Carasi (pseudonym) can and should be merely mentioned here, but not edited [60].

In addition and according to Freller it may be quite possible that the entire report on Malta by Carasi might have served the purpose of discrediting SMOM, and consequently could be classified as tendentious.[61]

In contrast to the above another source shall supplement the Bedford edition. In order to show that the rules found in the *Notizia* have been drawn up on the basis of an older set of regulations, this will be edited anew in the appendix. It originates from the second volume of the English version of the great history oeuvre on the Order, published 1728 by René Aubert de Vertot (called abbé Vertot) [61]. Vertot had become the official historiographer of SMOM. His original version of the history of the Order had been published in French language in Paris already in 1727. The source part of 196 pages, which appears to be more like an appendix, has the title *The old and new Statutes of the Order of St. John of Jerusalem, translated from Edition of Borgoforte, A.D. M,DC,LXXVI. By Order of the Chapter of the Great Priory of France.* In former times it was a peculiarity of the Maltensic (= referring to SMOM) legislation, that customary law regulations were placed first. These were followed by rules, which were based on decisions of earlier Chapters General (Legislative Assembly of the Order). These regulations were individually titled with the name of the respective Grandmaster who had presided over the particular Chapter. Then the majority of the rules followed. All parts concerning the hospital matters will be repeated here.

Reaching the end of this introduction I would like to return to the frontispiece right at the beginning. This title page shows the Patron of the Order, Saint John, in a fur garment - which is so typical for him - holding the crucifix stave adorned with an indistinct piece of cloth possibly depicting the flag of the Order. John is standing in a hospital which originates in medieval or early modern times; we may well assume this building is depicting the hospital of the Order of Malta. This is actually a partial view of a title page carried out as a copperplate engraving with a multitude of motives which are dominating the presentation. The volume - called the *Statuta Hospitalis Hierusalem* – contains the Statutes of the Order, which were reprinted several times during the ruling of Grandmaster Verdale during the fifteen eighties [63].

Down to modern times - today rather as a photographic image in context with book illustrations - medical institutions of SMOM are usually depicted with patients and *Malitensic* personnel. This is also the case with the copper etchings reproduced in this volume. However, the frontispiece piece shows only St. John and meticulously made beds for the sick: in other words: a hospital totally without any "Servants and Slaves of our esteemed patients (Messrs. Sick)" and actually without any sick person at all. A peculiar constellation for a Hospitaller Order! Is this perhaps a way of pointing out that the escort by the Order for the Pilgrims from and to Jerusalem in the Holy Land was so effective that consequently the declining number of injured persons due to the frequent armed holdups decreased the number of patients (Prevention is better than cure)? Or is the intention to portray as an allegory the (utopian) aim of the Order? In other words: after the patients have been cured due to the good medical attention, the beds in the wards remain empty? Though the beatified Gerhard had evidently renounced this idea already with: "Our Brotherhood will be everlasting, because the soil in which the plant is rooted, is the misery of the world, ...". Also a third interpretation might be imaginable: The print shows St. John in his typical pointing gesture, however, with only two fingers pointing inside - as it were with the hand of vow. The hand points to the oncoming Redeemer, who so often and in manifold ways announces the kingship and kingdom of God as "imminent" (Mark 1:15) and every now and then shows this by means of healing of the sick. Under such circumstances the ward beds in the hospital of the SMOM in the Kingdom of God would be permanently empty and doctors and nurses superfluous. Which ever interpretation may be the correct one, the illustration is to such a degree of expressive evidence that it was chosen as title etching also for this publication, just as formerly for Wienand's work.[64]

Wolf-Dieter Barz, Ingrid Kidder

SELECTIVE BIBLIOGRAPHY

Sovereign Military Order of Malta (general, monographs only)

Barber, Malcolm (ed.): The Military Orders (vol. I), Fighting for the Faith and Caring for the Sick, Aldershot et alt. 1994. – **Nicholson, Helen** (ed.): The Military Orders (vol. II), Welfare and Warfare, Aldershot et alt. 1998.

Blondy, Alain: L'Ordre de Malte au XVIII siècle, des dernières splendeurs à la ruine, Paris 2002.

Cassar, Paul: The Holy Infirmary of the Knights of St. John, la Sacra Infermeria, 3rd ed., Valletta 2005.

Cassar, Paul: Medical History of Malta, London 1964 (1965).

Cavaliero, Roderick : The Last of the Crusaders, the Knights of St. John and Malta in the Eighteenth Century, London 1960.

Clark, Robert M.: The Evangelical Knights of St. John, a History of the Bailiwick of Brandenburg of the Knightly Order of St. John of the Hospital at Jerusalem, known as the Johanniter Order, Dallas 2003.

Critien, A(ttilio): Holy Infirmary Sketches, Malta 1948.

Demurger, Alain: Die Ritter des Herrn, Geschichte der geistlichen Ritterorden, München 2003.

Freller, Thomas: Die Johanniter, vom Kreuzritter zum Samariter, die Geschichte des Malteserordens, Gernsbach 2012.

Freller, Thomas: Malta, the Order of St. John, Malta 2010.

Hirschberg, Ruth Maria: Hospitäler und Heilmethoden der Johanniter, ein geschichtlicher Überblick von den ersten Anfängen in Jerusalem bis zum großen Hospital auf Malta, 2002, http://www.brandenburg1260.de/hospital1.html (called up last 10th March, 2013).

Hume, Edgar Erskine: Medical work of the Knights Hospitallers of Saint John of Jerusalem, Baltimore 1940.

Karmon, Yehuda: Die Johanniter und Malteser, Ritter und Samariter, die Wandlungen des Ordens vom heiligen Johannes, München 1987.

Mallia-Milanes, Victor (Ed.): Hospitaller Malta 1530-1798, Studies on Early Modern Malta and the Order of St. John of Jerusalem, Msida (Malta) 1993.

Mitchel, Piers D.: Medicine in the Crusades. Warfare, Wounds and the Medieval Surgeon, Cambridge University Press 2004.

Pappalardo, Ignazio : Storia sanitaria dell'Ordine Gerosolimitano di Malta dalle origini al presente, Roma 1958.

Prokopowski, Rudolf: Ordre Souverain et Militaire Jérosolymitain de Malte, Citta del Vaticano 1950.

Riley-Smith, Jonathan (Ed.): Hospitallers, the History of the Order of St. John, London et alt. 1999.

Sainty, Guy S.: The Orders of St. John, the History, Structure, Membership and the modern Role of the five Hospitaller orders of Saint John of Jerusalem, New York 1991.

Savona-Ventura, Ch(arles): Civil Hospitals in Malta
http://www.oocities.org/hotsprings/2615/medhist/hospital2.htm (called up last 10th March, 2013).

Savona-Ventura, Charles: Knight Hospitaller Medicine in Malta, 1530-1798, San Gwann (Malta) 2004.

Scarabelli, Giovanni: La Sacra Infermeria a Malta nel Settecento, Milano 2009.

Schermerhorn, Elizabeth Wheeler: Malta of the Knights, London 1929, (reprint) 1978.

Sire, H(enry) J. A.: The Knights of Malta, New Haven et alt. 1994 (1996).

Staehle, Ernst: Die Malteserritter, Schild der Christenheit im Mittelmeer, Gnas 2002.

Steeb, Christian et alt. (ed.) : Der Souveräne Malteser-Ritter-Orden in Österreich, Graz 1999.

Waldstein-Wartenberg, Berthold: Rechtsgeschichte des Malteserordens, Wien et alt. 1969.

Wienand, Adam (ed.): Der Johanniterorden, der Malteserorden, der ritterliche Orden des hl. Johannes vom Spital zu Jerusalem, seine Geschichte, seine Aufgaben, 3rd. ed., Köln 1988.

Zwehl, Hans Karl von: Nachrichten über die Armen- und Krankenfürsorge des Ordens vom Hospital des heil(igen) Johannes von Jerusalem oder Souveränen Malteser-Ritterordens, Rom 1911.

Zwehl, Hans Karl von: Über die Caritas im Johanniter-Malteser-Orden, eine Studie, Essen [1928].

FOOTNOTES

Footnotes - Spiritual foreword

1. The Bible in the translation by D. Martin Luther, revised edition 1912, edited by Württembergische Bibelanstalt. (For the English text the translator used The New Testament in Today's English Version, third edition, Days Inn, American Bible Society, 1966, 1971).

2. **Rödel, Walter G.:** Helfen im Zeichen des achtspitzigen Kreuzes. Source: Rittergesellschaft Rubikon, 2005 annual edition.

3. **Kaehne, H. von:** lecture entitled "The hospital charter of Roger de Molin of 14 March 1181 for the Hospital of Saint John in Jerusalem." A Mühltal 1999, to be obtained from the Hessian chapter of the Order of Saint John.

4. The Great Hospital at Valetta in 1726, from the Italian original preserved in the archives of Malta. The regulations of the old hospital of the knights of Saint John at Valetta, William Blackwood and Sons, Edinburgh and London 1882. [Other title of Bedford's work edited here]

5. Membership in the Order of Malta, Rules and commentaries, Prince and Grand Master Fra' Matthew Festhing, 18 February 2011, Rome 2011.

6. Wikipedia entry for the Order of Saint John.

Footnotes - The developments covering the Sacra Infermeria at la Valletta

1 **Barz, Wolf-Dieter**: Friedrich v. Schiller und der Johanniter-/Malteserorden, Schillers historisches und staatstheoretisches Interesse an der Ordensgeschichte, in: Der Johanniterorden in Baden-Württemberg, No. 99 (1999), p. 18-22.

2 **Zedler, Johann Heinrich**: Grosses vollständiges Universal-Lexicon aller Wissenschaften und Künste, welche bißhero durch menschlichen Verstand und Witz erfunden und verbessert worden ...., vol. 19, Halle et alt. 1739, *Malteser-Ritter*, col. 772-779 (*772*).

3 **Hirschberg, Ruth Maria**: Hospitäler und Heilmethoden der Johanniter von den ersten Anfängen in Jerusalem bis zum großen Hospital auf Malta (part 1), p. 4, http://www.brandenburg1260.de/hospital1html (called up last 13th March, 2013). - Cfr. **Dock, Lavinia L.** and **Stewart, Isabel M.**: A short history of nursing, from the Earliest Times to the Present Day, 4th ed., New York et alt. 1938, p.62.

4 **Delaville LeRoulx, Joseph**: Cartulaire générale de l'ordre des hospitaliers de S. Jean de Jérusalem, 1100-1310, vol. 1: 1100-1200, Paris 1894, No. 29, p. 30. – **Bremer, Jörg**: Im Dienste der Nächstenliebe, Malteser und Johanniter feiern im Vatikan ihr neunhundertjähriges Bestehen, in: Frankfurter Allgemeine Zeitung, No. 35, 11.2.2013, p. 9, (1113 is not the year of foundation of the Maltese Order, and the document of Pope Paschalis II dated 15th February, 1113, is not a foundation memorandum. However, this document constitutes an important step towards the development of the hospital community towards an Order in a canonical sense.).

5 **Klement, Katja**: Gottes Gastgeber, die Ritter des Hospitals von Jerusalem, die vatikanische Handschrift Vat. Lat. 4852, (with transcription, translation and facsimile), Norderstedt 2010, p. 33.

6 Gollwitzer-Voll, Woty: Christus Medicus, Heilung als Mysterium, Interpretationen eines alten Christusnamens und dessen Bedeutung in der Praktischen Theologie, Paderborn et alt. 2007.

7 **Barz, Wolf-Dieter**: In Marburg, der Johanniterorden als Rechtsnachfolger der hl. Elisabeth?, in: Der Johanniterorden in Baden-Württemberg, No. 116 (2007), pp. 15-18.

8 Quoted at **Overath, Joseph**: Dem Kranken dienen wie Christus selbst, Dokumente zum christlichen Verständnis von Krankheit und ihrer Pflege in Geschichte und Gegenwart, Frankfurt am Main et alt. 1983, p. 91.

9 **Dock, Lavinia L.** and **Stewart, Isabell**: see No. 3, p. 64, 65.

10 **Ellul, Michael**: The Valletta Holy Infimary, the building and the institution, in: **Marconi, Nicoletta** (ed.): Valletta, città, architettura e costruzione sotto il segno della fede e della guerra, Roma 2011, pp. 157-177 (*166*).

11 Ibid., p.164.

12 **Feucht, Gerhart; Leidwein, Brigitte E.**: Die Hospitalität im Souveränen Malteser-Ritter-Orden, in: **Steeb, Christian** et alt. (ed.): Der Souveräne Malteser-Ritter-Orden, Graz 1999, pp. 323-360 (*332*).

13 **Freller, Thomas**: Ein Hospital als Symbol des Staates, die Sacra Infermeria auf Malta, in: Pharmazeutische Zeitung, Nr. 13, vol. 142, 1997, pp. 11-15 (*14*).

14 **Freller, Thomas**: ibid.

15 **Cassar, Paul**: A medical Service for Slaves in Malta during the Rule of the Order of St. John of Jerusalem, in: Medical History, vol. 12, 1968, pp. 270-277 (*271*).

16 **Staehle, Ernst**: Die Malteserritter, Schild der Christenheit im Mittelmeer, Gnas 2002, S. 92. – **Freller, Thomas**: „The very Glory of Malta", das Ordenshospital „La Sacra Infermeria" auf Malta als Denkmal früh-neuzeitlicher Karitas und Medizingeschichte, in: Medizinhistorisches Journal, internationale Vierteljahresschrift für Wissenschaftsgeschichte, vol. 30, 1995, pp. 51-59.

17 **Critien, Attilio**: Holy Infirmary Sketches, Malta 1946, p. III.

18 **Harding, W(illiam D.)**: Foreword, in: No. 17, p. VI.

19 **Freller, Thomas**: No. 13, pp. 11-15 (*11*).

20 **Freller, Thomas**: No. 16, p. 52.

21 **Jetter, Dieter**: Das europäische Hospital, von der Spätantike bis 1800, 2. ed., Köln 1987, p. 90.

22 **Vella, Andrew P.**: The University of Malta, a bicentenary memorial, Malta 1969, p. 42 et seq.

23 **Freller, Thomas**: No. 13, p. 14.

24 **Ittner, Joseph Albrecht von**: Ueber die Gesetze und Verfassung der Maltheser-Ordens Republick nebst einer Abhandlung über die Unanwendbarkeit der Oesterreichischen Amortizationsgesetze auf die Mitglieder derselben, Carlsruhe 1797. – When refering to the Maltese Order Schiller uses either the term „political corporate body" or the term „monastic-knightly state"; **Schiller, Friedrich von**: Vorrede, in: **N(iethammer, Friedrich Immanuel)**: Geschichte des Maltheserordens nach Vertot, vol. 1, pp. I-XVI, (*XI, XII*).

25 http://www.regalis.com/malta/deedCharles.pdf (called up last 16th March, 2013).

26 **Serra, H.P.**: Un Etat sans Etat, in: Archives diplomatiques et consulaire, 1943, pp. 189-194.

27 **Reinhardt, Heinrich**: Der Personalstaat, Profil einer neuen Staatsform, Bern et. alt. 1999.

28 http://www.orderofmalta.int/medical-and-humanitarian-activities/55/the-mission-to-help-the-sick-and-the-needy/?lang=en (called up last 16th June, 2013).

29 **Clark, Robert M.**: The Evangelical Knights of St. John, a history of the Bailiwick of Brandenburg of the Knightly Order of St. John of the Hospital at Jerusalem, known as the Johanniter Orden, Dallas 2003. – **Sainty, Guy S.**: The Orders of St. John, the History, Structure, Membership and modern Role of the five Hospitallers Orders of Saint John of Jerusalem, New York 1991.

30 **Blondy, Alain**: L'Ordre de Malte au XVIII siècle, des dernières splendeurs à la ruine, Paris 2002.

31 **Ballestrem, Carl Wolfgang von**: Die Hospitalität der Malteser heute, in: Wienand, Adam et alt.(ed.): Der Johanniter-Orden, der Malteser-Orden, der ritterliche Orden des hl. Johannes vom Spital zu Jerusalem, seine Geschichte, seine Aufgaben, 3rd ed., Köln 1988, pp. 563-574.

32 **Hume, Edgar Erskine**: Medical work of the Knights Hospitallers of Saint John of Jerusalem, Baltimore 1940, p. 136. – A second publication by Humes, i.e. a monographic reprint of an essay with the same title has emerged from a series of lectures, and describes the hospitality of SMOM from the beginning up to its time on Rhodes.

33 **Camilleri, Joseph**: History of Nursing in Malta (part 2), the Knights of Malta, 1530-1798, pp. 1-5 (*1*), http://www.sahha.gov.mt/showdoc.aspx?id=37&filesource=4&file=2_knightsofmalta.pdf

34 **Schiller, Friedrich von**: see No. **10b**, pp. 9 et seq. – Cfr. **Zwehl, Hans Karl von**: Über die Caritas im Johanniter- Malteser-Orden seit seiner Gründung, eine Studie, Essen [1928], pp. 30 et seq.; 37 et seq.

35 Constitution donnée par Napoleon aux habitans de l' isle d'Elbe [Paris ca. 1815].

36 Personal note by Professor Dr. **William Zammit**, Malta, Spring 2013.

37 **Ballestrem, Carl Wolfgang von**: Die Hospitalität des Ordens, in: Wienand, Adam et alt. (ed.): Der Johanniterorden, der Malteserorden, der ritterliche Orden des hl. Johannes vom Spital zu Jerusalem, seine Geschichte, seine Aufgaben, 3rd ed., Köln 1988, pp. 257-273 (*269*).

38 **Barz, Wolf-Dieter**: Pinto's principality or the story of the Melitensic-Maltese crown – an addendum to Cachia, in: Sacra Militia, the journal of the history of the Order of St. John, iss. 11, 2012, pp. 47-50.

39 For examples see: **Grima, Michel-Angiolo**: Due relazioni medico-anatomiche, una dell' apertura del cadavere della già illustrissima signora Leonora Montauti-Mancini ...., Malta 1764. – Codice del Sacro Militare Ordine Gerosolimitano ..., Malta 1782. – Del dritto municipale di Malta, nuova compilatione con diverse altre costituzioni, Malta 1784.

40 **Zammit**, William: Printing in Malta 1642-1839, its cultural role from inception to the granting of freedom of the press, Malta 2008, p. 39.

41 Personal note by Professor Dr. **William Zammit**, dated Malta 26th March 2013.

42 Ibid.

43 **Ballestrem, Carl Wolfgang von**: No. 37, p. 270.

44 **Zwehl, Hans Karl von**: Nachrichten über die Armen- und Krankenfürsorge des Ordens vom Hospital des heil(igen) Johannes von Jerusalem oder Souveränen Malteser-Ritterordens, Rom 1911, p. 35, fn. 2.

45 **Dock, Lavinia L.** and **Stewart, Isabel M.**: No. 3, p. 62.

46 **Micallef, Antonio**: Lectures on the Statutes of the Sacred Order of St. John of Jerusalem at the University (of Studies) of Malta 1792, ed. by **Barz, Wolf-Dieter,** and **Galea, Michael**, Karlsruhe 2012.

47 **Bedford, William Kirkpatrick Riland**: The Regulations of the old Hospital of the Knights of St. John at Val(l)etta, from a copy printed at Rome, and preserved in the Archives of Malta with a Translation, Introduction, and Notes explanatory of the Hospital Work of the Order, Edinburgh et alt. 1882. – **Bedford, William Kirkpatrick Riland**: Malta and the Knights Hospitallers, London 1894. – **Bedford, William Kirkpatrick Riland** and **Holbeche, Richard**: The Order of the Hospital of St. John of Jerusalem, being a history of the English Hospitallers of St. John, their Rise and Progress, London 1902.

48 **Scarabelli, Giovanni**: La Sacra Infermeria a Malta nel settencento, 2nd ed., Milano 2008, p. 13 et seq.

49 Karlsruher Virtueller Katalog, http://www.ubka.uni-karlsruhe.de/kvk.html, (called up last 16th February, 2013).

50 **Hume, Edgar Erskine**: No. 32, p. 141.

51 Even as late as the last centry Romano Guardine (1885-1968) appears to reflect on such thoughts: "Dazu sieht Er [i.e. Jesus] das Leid viel zu tief, viel zu weit drunten in den Wurzeln des Daseins, eins mit Sünde und Gottfremdheit." –„In this context He [i.e. Jesus] considers the pain far too low, far too embroiled within the roots of existence, being at one with sin and godlessness." Quoted at **Overath, Joseph**: see No. 8, p. 83.

52 **Wienand, Adam**: Die Hospitalkirche der Johanniter als Bautypus, in: Wienand, Adam et alt. (ed.) Der Johanniterorden, der Malteserorden, der ritterliche Orden des hl. Johannes vom Spital zu Jerusalem, seine Geschichte, seine Aufgaben, 3rd ed., Köln 1988, pp. 409-421, *(419-420)*. – **Slenczka, Ruth**: Ein mittelalterliches Hospital in Nieder-Weisel, Überlegungen zur Funktion der

Doppelstöckigkeit der Ordenskirche, in: Jahrbuch der Hessischen Kirchengeschichtlichen Vereinigung, Vol. 59 (2008) (Johanniter in Hessen, 800 Jahre diakonischer Auftrag) pp. 44-64. - **Gließner, Michael**: Die Johanniterkirche in Nieder-Weisel, Speyer 2000.

53 **Lagleder, Gerhard Tonque**: Die Ordensregel der Johanniter/Malteser, die geistlichen Grundlagen des Johanniter-/Malteserordens, mit einer Edition und Übersetzung der drei ältesten Regelhandschriften, St. Ottilien, 1983. – **Klement, Katja**, No. 5.

54 **Wood, G.S.** (rev. by **Potier, Joanne**): Bedford, William Kirkpatrick Riland, in: Matthew, H.C.G. et alt. (ed.): Oxford dictionary of national biography, from the earliest times to the year 2000, vol. 4, Oxford 2004, p. 778.

55 http://www.orderofmalta.int/history/802/orders-of-st-john/?lang=en http://www.orderofmalta.int/history/813/mimic-orders-of-malta/?lang=en

56 **Vann, Theresa M.**: The Archives and Library of the Sacra Infermeria, Malta, in: **Bowers, Barbara S.** (ed.): The Medieval Hospital and Medical Practice, Aldershot 2007, pp. 19-40, (*23, 28*).

57 **Howard, John**: An account of the principal Lazarettos in Europe, with various papers relative to the plague, together with further observations on some foreign prisons and hospitals, and additional remarks on present state of those in Great Britain and Ireland, London 1789, pp. 58-61.

58 **John, Howard** Wikipedia
http://en.wikipedia.org/wiki/John_Howard_%28prison_reformer%29

59 **Wesel, Uwe**: Geschichte des Rechts in Europa, von den Griechen bis zum Vertrag von Lissabon, München 2010, pp. 361-364.

60 **Carasi, M.** [pseud.]: The Order of Malta exposed or a voyage to Malta, containing historical, philosophical, and critical observations on the actual situation of the State of the Knights of Malta and their morals, also containing descriptions of the nature, products of the island, and the customs of its inhabitants, translation and introduction by Thomas Freller, Malta 2010, pp. 144-152.

61 **Freller, Thomas**: Introduction, a scandalous book and its background, in: see No. 59, pp. 7-20.

62 **Vertot, abbé de (René Aubert de):** The history oft the Knights Hospitallers of St. John of Jerusalem, styled afterwards, the Knights of Rhodes, and at present, the Knights of Malta, vol. 2., London 1728.

63 Statv(u)ta Hospitalis Hierv(u)salem, (Roma 1588), title-leaf.

64 **Wienand, Adam** et alt. (ed.): Der Johanniterorden, der Malteserorden, der ritterliche Orden des hl. Johannes vom Spital zu Jerusalem, seine Geschichte, seine Aufgaben, 3d. ed., Köln 1988, frontispiece.

Part II

The Great ward of the Sacred Infirmary or Hospital of the Knights of Saint John at Valletta, Malta, as it appeared in the seventeenth century.

From the German history of the Hospitallers, printed in Augsburg in 1650.

There are shown the beds of the sick with mosquito-nets and Knights in attendance on the patients. In the foreground a funeral ceremony.

THE
REGULATIONS OF THE OLD HOSPITAL

OF THE

KNIGHTS OF ST JOHN

AT VALETTA

From a Copy Printed at Rome, and preserved in
the Archives of Malta

WITH A

TRANSLATION, INTRODUCTION, AND NOTES EXPLANATORY
OF THE HOSPITAL WORK OF THE ORDER

BY THE

REV. W. K. R. BEDFORD

ONE OF THE CHAPLAINS OF THE ORDER OF ST JOHN IN ENGLAND

WILLIAM BLACKWOOD AND SONS
EDINBURGH AND LONDON
MDCCCLXXXII

TO THE

COUNCIL OF THE ORDER OF ST JOHN
IN ENGLAND

THIS SMALL CONTRIBUTION TO THE HISTORY OF THEIR
PREDECESSORS' WORK IS DEDICATED BY THEIR CON-
FRÉRE

THE EDITOR

PREFACE.

No relics can be so interesting to Hospitallers as the traces of the special work and purpose of their Order. If, by the indefatigable exertions of our Secretary, the English Langue is ever enabled again to occupy a hospice at Jerusalem, it will be a matter of high satisfaction to know that we shall be on the very traces of the founders of the Order, whose first Grand Master, Gerard, presided over the House of Refuge - erected, as some say, by John Hyrcanus, who bequeathed to it his name, but more probably by Charlemagne, or by the Abbot of the Augustinian convent of Naples, and dedicated either to St John the Baptist, or to that Bishop of Alexandria whose good deeds procured him canonisation as St John the Almoner. Which of these statements is correct, or what the exact position of Gerard himself, whether monk or soldier, is now a mere antiquarian speculation, though the folios of the last century are full of pages of learning on the subject. It is more important to trace the fact that while we have scarcely any details of the construction or management of the hospitals of the Order prior to its establishment in Malta, we are assured that wherever the fluctuating fortunes of the knights led them to find a home, and wherever their branch foundations were erected, their hospital work was as distinctly recognised as their religious or their military character. So that at length it seemed as if St John, like St Vitus and St Anthony, would have his name appropriated to some one of the painful maladies which afflict humanity.[1]

When the Knights of St John, under their Grand Master Philip Villiers Delisle Adam, took possession of their future home at Malta, they found there a hospital in the ancient capital of Citta Vecchia. The foundation is still in existence, under the control of the Government, as a hospital, and is called Santo Spirito; but having been entirely rebuilt and remodelled by Grand Master Manoel de Vil-

---

[1] See Note A, page 43.

hena, it contains no traces of its original condition. The Order no doubt found it necessary to have a building nearer to their own headquarters, and in the Citta Vittoriosa or Borgo, which lies behind Fort St Angelo, the scanty remains of their first Maltese hospital may be seen, incorporated with more modern buildings, used as a nunnery. An exterior doorway, having pomegranates conspicuous among its ornaments, and an interior arch - of which a good account, with an engraving, is furnished in a magazine[2] published some years back at Valetta - are the only architectural relics of interest. Indeed, in 1575, less than fifty years after their arrival, the hospital was transferred to the new city of Valetta; and, by an unfortunate choice of situation, the south-eastern side of the promontory, close to the entrance of the great harbour, was selected - being the lowest part of the new city, near the outlet of the sewer, and exposed to the sirocco wind, while sheltered by adjacent buildings from the wholesome breezes which play from the other points of the compass. The Report of the Barrack and Hospital Commission of 1863, which will be found in the Note, sweepingly condemns it;[3] yet as a monument of grand architecture, and for splendour of equipment and service, it was long unrivalled, and still maintains a deep interest. The first erection seems to have been the great hall, now divided by partitions (which do not reach more than half its height) into several wards, but containing, under one roof, a room 503 feet long, 34 feet 10 inches broad, and 30 feet 6 inches high. The beams of the roof appear to be of red deal, although common report states Sicilian chestnut to be the wood employed in their construction. The apartment at right angles also formed part of the same great hall, though now divided by another partition of about 12 feet in height. There seems to have been a communication with the sea by means of a vaulted passage, a portion of which, cut off by rough masonry, was brought to light last spring during the sewerage excavations. At the end of this large apartment is a small ora-

---

[2] See Note B, page 44.
[3] See Note C, page 44.

tory, and there are traces of an altar (as shown in the engraving, from a German account of the Order published in Augsburg in 1650), above which now hangs a large picture representing the reception of the hand of St John by the Grand Master D'Aubusson. All down the wall, on the sea-side of the apartment, are little recesses, which were used as latrines in former days. The windows were high and small, so that the apartment was (and is even with its additional windows) very dull and somewhat close. The dreariness of the room was relieved in former times by tapestries and pictures - the work of Matteo Preti and of others. To those who look at sanitation with the eyes of the seventeenth century, there is nothing but admiration to be given to the costly - nay, lavish - arrangements and service of the hospital. We find Teonge, the English man-of-war's chaplain, who has left us an amusing diary of his voyages in Charles II.'s time, loud in its praise; and Sandys, a few years before, selects for especial commendation the canopies of the beds, shown in the German engraving - very like the mosquito-curtains at present in use in Valetta - and the fortnightly supply of clean linen! Howard's perspicuous sense of what was really required in a well-ordered hospital no doubt detected many abuses at the time of his visit about a hundred years ago; but one point which he selects for comment - viz., that many of the inmates had pewter dishes only instead of silver - indicates a want of knowledge of the Regulations, which expressly prescribe pewter for the *gente di catena,* or criminal class of patients.[4] That the hospital was a constant source of care to the Order, is apparent by the many additions made from time to time to its buildings and revenues, and by the fact that with decaying funds caused by the loss of revenue,[5] and the unlucky result of their compact with the Antonine Order, their expenditure upon the hospital never relaxed; and even down to the year 1796,

---

[4] See Note D, page 48.
[5] See Note H, page 55.

the means of improving its efficiency was the subject of serious consideration in the Councils of the Order.[6]

The buildings were extended in 1662, and again by Grand Master Perellos, who erected the front towards Strada Mercanti in 1712. But the obliteration of the arms of the Grand Hospitallers from 1683 to 1701, at the point where an arch has been broken through to connect the new work with the old quarters of the superintending officers, would seem to indicate that some portion of the work at least was commenced at an earlier date.[7] In Perellos's time, also, the Chapel of the Holy Sacrament was erected opposite the ward for the dying. In 1774 a large sum was spent on repairs, and in 1780 a very injudicious addition was made of certain rooms and passages now used as stores.[8] The total number of halls or wards in 1796 was stated at twelve, with four supplementary chambers.[9]

The present buildings of the hospital embrace, on the side opening from Strada Mercanti, a quadrangle 90 feet by 88 feet, in the centre of which is a fountain decorated with pears carved in stone - the arms of Grand Master Perellos. In this court is the dispensary, containing curious old earthenware jars and metal fittings, including a pestle and mortar of bell-metal, with Perellos's arms again engraved. Here are also a library, and quarters for medical officers. In one corner (for the first quadrangle is at an angle of forty-five to the rest of the building) is a flight of stairs leading up to the ward where the arms of the Hospitallers are emblazoned, and another staircase descending to a corridor which leads to the great ward of the ancient hospital, through a quadrangle, at a level of 35 feet below the entrance, 130 feet 6 inches by 84 feet. The intermediate space is occupied by a triangular court, the rooms in which are appropriated to the sick of the Malta Fencibles Artillery.

---

[6] See Note E, page 51.
[7] See Note F, page 52.
[8] See Note G, page 54.
[9] See Note H, page 55.

The other traces of the hospital system of the knights are to be found in a building known as the Camerata, originally the linen-store of the hospital, and its laundry. The cemetery of the old hospital is now part of the site of the House of Incurables, where many of the bones, once interred, there, are to be seen in architectural figures upon the walls of a subterranean chapel. Hard by is the church of Nibbia, containing the tomb of the knight of that name, who was a founder of the hospital in 1574, and died 1619.

The Book of Regulations, now translated, is preserved, with a few other accounts of the last century relating to the hospital, in the public archives at Valetta. No attempt has been made to do more than give a literal translation of the quaint phraseology of the original; nor has it been thought advisable to attempt to modernise the spelling, or to correct the possible errors of the typography of so curious a relic of hospital economy, embodying, no doubt, the details of the system in use from the very foundation of the building in 1575. It gives a very full and interesting detail, not only of the routine of the hospital management, but also of the system of dispensaries in the affiliated towns, and of doles or stated pittances of food or money, which continued to be distributed even after the English occupation. It would appear, from other records, that in 1796 a new system of regulations was about to be introduced. It was then proposed to give the dispenser 57 *scudi* a-month, and to allow him six assistants; thirty-eight servants being provided for the general work of the hospital. We have a good report of it from the French traveller St Priest at that time.[10] But the downfall of the Order entirely altered its position and objects. Should it now cease to be used as a military hospital, it is to be hoped that the building, at least, will be spared as a grand relic of charitable magnificence.

---

[10] See Note I, page 55.

CONTENTS

REGULATIONS OF THE HOLY INFIRMARY OF MALTA 71

REGULATIONS FOR THE SICK POOR OF MALTA 97

NOTES 114

ORDER OF ST JOHN OF JERUSALEM IN ENGLAND 1881. 135

TAVOLA PER L'INFERMIA. 140

TAVOLA PER LA CARICA DELLI COMMISSARJ
DELLE POVERE INFERME. 146

TABLE FOR THE INFIRMARY 149

TABLE FOR THE OFFICE OF THE COMMISSIONERS
OF THE POOR INFIRM WOMEN. 155

View of the great Ward of the knights of
St. John in Valletta   *Frontispice*

Sections of Part of the Hospital ward 112

Ground Plan 113

NOTIZIA
DELLA
SACRA INFERMERIA,
E
DELLA CARICA
DELLI COMMISSARJ
Delle Povere Inferme

IN ROMA.
Nella Stamperia di Rocco Bernabo, l'Anno del Giubileo MDCCXXV.
CON LICENZA DE' SUPERIORI.

REGOLAMENTO DELLA SACRA INFERMERIA DI MALTA

(REGULATIONS OF THE HOLY INFIRMARY OF MALTA)

REGOLAMENTO DELLA SACRA INFERMERIA DI MALTA.

Il Superiore, e Capo, della Sacra Infermeria è L'Eminentissimo, e Reverendissimo Gran Maestro, che s'intitola Magnus Magister Hospitalis Hierusalem.
Il Grand Ospedaliere Capo della lingua di Francia per sua antica preminenza presiede nell'Infermeria, al buon, governo, della quale invigila.
L'Infermiere è un cavaliere professo, al di cui zelo è raccomandata la cura dell'infermie, i quale deve provedere, di letto, secondo la loro condizione, e bisogno; e abita nell'Infermeria in appartamento separato. La mattina a buon'ora fa suonare la visita, nella quale interviene per far'osservare con la dovuta carità delli medici l'infermi, e acciò gli sia ordinato il bisognevole: venuto per il tempo del desinare fa suonare la mangia per avisare tutti gl'officiali, e assiste alla medesima acciò ogni letto abia la pitanza ordinatali, e ognuno de'subalterni faccia il suo, dovere; e lo stesso fa la sera nella visita, e cena. Deve sopra tutto far'osservare la dovuta quiete, e perciò, di notte suol spesso visitare tutti e letti, e sale per la vigilanza delle guardie, lumi, ed altro. È' sua inspezione di far serrare alla solita ora di notte le porte, e portone dell'Infermeria, e procurare, che tutti gl'officiali destinati siano ritirati e a tale effetto ha l'autorità di licenziare, e mettere i guardiani, o siano servi, e gastigarli nella forma che meritano, mancando alla polizia, e custodia de'malati.

REGULATIONS OF THE HOLY INFIRMARY OF MALTA.

The Superior, or Head, of the Holy Infirmary, is the Most Eminent and Very Reverend the Grand Master, who is styled Magnus Magister Hospitalis Hierusalem.

The Grand Hospitaller, Head of the French Langue, presides, by virtue of his ancient precedence, over the Infirmary, and attends to its welfare.

The Infirmarían is a professed knight, to whose zeal the care of the sick is Intrusted, whom he must provide with beds, according to their condition and need. He resides in a separate apartment in the Infirmary. Early in the morning he has the bell rung for the visitation, at which he is present, to see that the sick are carefully attended to by the physicians, and that what is necessary is ordered for them. The time for dining arrived, he has the dinner-bell rung to summon all the officials, and he is present at the same to make sure that each bed is supplied with the proper allowance, and that each of the subordinates does his duty; and he does the same in the evening at the visitation and supper. Above everything, he must have perfect quietness observed, and therefore he must often visit the beds at night, and the wards, to look after the warders, lights, &c. It is his duty to see that the doors and great gate of the Infirmary are locked at the usual hour at night, and to take care that all the officers on duty have retired; and to effect this, he has authority to dismiss and appoint the warders or servants, and to punish them as they deserve should they fail in attention to and care of the sick.

Ha in oltre cura speciale della casa, detta la Falanga, nella quale la Sacra Religione fa nodrire i poveri bambini esposti, con la seperazione conveniente dell'uno e l'altro sesso sotto la cura di tré donne da bene, ed attempate, facendoli prima munire del santo battesimo, e per allattare in casa di balie, e educare nella miglior forma, procurando, di collocarli, adulti che siano, o in matrimonio, ó al servizio di persone onorate, e per allevare parte di zitelle con la dovuta pietà si riducono in un conservatorio dove se li paga il necessario mantenimento.

Per l'economia poi si nominano dall'Eminentissimo Gran Maestro diece cavalieri professi probihomini, detti volgarmente Prodomi, che devono provedere del bisognevole l'infermi invigilando sopra la qualità, e quantità delle pitanze, sopra la destribuzione de'medicamenti, e di tutte le vettovaglie, e commestibili necessarj. Devono di più notare la spesa d'ogni giorno, e il consumo di tutto ciò, che se usa nell'Infermeria, firmando, di mano propria tutti i pagamenti. Provedono di quotidiane elemosine molti poveri incurabili, e inabili a procacciarsi il vitto, e dispensano ad altri, oltre quel, che rimane nelle caldare molta quantità di consumato, e pasta che a bella posta se fa cucinare ogni giorno; di più una gran parte di lenzuola usate, e coperte, che si danno a povere donne e molte legature, e bastoni per li stropj. Provedendo di balie alle quali contribuiscono mesata, e vestiario per i poveri fanciulli esposti à' quali non allattando più, fanno somministrare il necessario vitto nel detto luogo della Falanga, e per fine invigilano sopra il buon governo di quelli, che pigliano le stuffe, o véro l'unzione mercuriale nel detto luogo separato dall'Ospedale.

L'armoriere suol'essere un fra serviente d'armi, al quale è consegnata tutta l'argenteria dell'Infermeria, che è per uso degl'infermi, per la sua polizia e sicurezza.

Vi è un'altro fra serviente d'armi, che si chiama scrivano dell'Abito, il quale ha' l'ispezzione di notare la spesa di tutta l'Infermeria nel libro maestro, che ogn'anno si consegna nella Rev. Camera del Coni: Tesoro. Accodisce nel tempo della mancia; e ha l'incompensa di stendere i testamenti, che fanno l'infermi, e questi dormono nell'Infermeria.

He has, besides, special charge of the house called La Falanga, where the Holy Religion brings up the Foundlings, with the proper separation of the sexes, under the charge of three good and elderly women, having them at first baptised, and provided with wet-nurses, educating them in the best manner, and settling them in life when grown up - either in marriage or in the service of respectable people; and, to bring up some of the girls with due devotion, they are sent to a convent, where their necessary maintenance is defrayed.

Two professed knights of integrity (commonly called *Prodomi)* are appointed by the Most Eminent the Grand Master, who must attend to the wants of the sick, looking after the quality and quantity of the allowances, the distribution of the medicines, and all necessary provisions and food. They must also note the daily expenses and consumption of things in the Infirmary, signing with their own hand the vouchers for payments.

They provide many poor incurables, who are incapable of providing for themselves, with daily alms, and distribute to others, in addition to what remains in the caldrons, a large quantity of soup and vermicelli, which is cooked on purpose every day; also a large number of old sheets and coverlets are given to poor women, and many bandages and crutches to cripples. They provide nurses, give them payment monthly, and clothing for the poor Foundlings, to whom, when they are weaned, they give the necessary food in the aforementioned place, La Falanga; and, finally, they superintend the management of the hot baths and mercurial anointing, which are in a separate ward of the Hospital.

The *Armoriere* is usually a *frà serviente d'armi,* to whom is intrusted all the silver plate of the Infirmary which is used for the sick, and he is responsible for its cleanliness and safe custody.

There is another *frà serviente d'armi* called "Clerk of the Habit," whose duty it is to register all the expenses of the Infirmary in the principal ledger, which is delivered every year to the Reverend Chamber of the Common Treasury. He is present at the time of the *mancia* (distribution of doles), and is intrusted to draw up the wills of the sick, and he lives in the Hospital.

Lo Scrivano de' Prodomi è un Secolare, il quale è sobbordinato alli Prodomi, notando tutto ciò, che concerne la carica de' medesimi nelli libri distinti, e hà la stanza nell'Infermeria.

Il Linciere è un Secolare, a chi sta consegnata tutta la biancheria, e masserizie, invigilando a farla ben biancheggiare, mutare e accomodare, secondo il bisogno al qual'effetto ha un servitore pagato, e molti schiavi per lavare, cucire e battere la lana de' materrazzi.

Il Bottigliere tiene in consegna tutto il vino, pane, oglio ed altro, che deve, dare secondo le polize de' Prodomi, e hà un ajutante pagato, e stanza nella Infermeria.

Lo Scivanello hà il carico di notare il mangiare, che ordinano i medici nella mancia, e consegnare le liste a Prodomi per poter questi in tempo próvedere il bisognevole.

Sieguono a questi due cuochi.

Compratore, e compagni, che próvedono tutta la carne per le pitanze, che non possono ricevere in cocina senza essere prima ben' osservate da' Prodomi.

Vi sono quattordici servi, che si chiamano guardiani, due de quali destinati per li cavalieri persone dell'Abito, e fanno le loro guardie di giorno e di notte per la custodia dell'infermi, al servizio de' quali devono accudire. Doppo di questi vengono due portieri che del continuo sono di guardia per la custodia delle porte.

Per agiuto poi della cucina, e de' guardiani per polire i vasi immondi, e altri bassi officj si eleggono dalla Prigione de' Schiavi 44 tra Cristiani, e Turchi per i quali vi è un'Infermeria particolare nella istessa prigione.

Ecclesiastici.

Per l'assistenza degl' infermi circa il spirituale, il capo è il Priore, il quale è un frà cappellano conventuale, che hà cura di far riconciliare tutti gl' infermi che entrano nell'Ospedale prima delle 24 ore, mentre altrimenti non si ricovererebbero, e invigila sopra l'amministrazione de' sacramenti, e assistenza de' moribondi per accudire a i quali in compagnia degl' altri fa le sue guardie, di notte e di giorno, e confessa li ammalati.

The Secretary of the *Prodomi* is a Secular, subordinate to them, noting everything concerning their work in separate books; and he has an apartment in the Infirmary.

The *Linciere* is a Secular, with whom is deposited all the linen and furniture (or household goods), and he must see that they are washed, changed, and mended, as may be necessary. For this he is allowed a paid servant, and several slaves to wash, sew, and beat the wool of the mattresses.

The *Bottigliere* takes charge of all the wine, bread, oil, &c., which he supplies according to the vouchers of the *Prodomi*. He has a paid assistant, and a room in the Infirmary.

The under Clerk has charge of noting the food prescribed by the doctors in the *mancia,* and of delivering the list to the *Prodomi,* that they may be able to provide in time what is necessary.

There are two cooks, a purveyor, and assistants, who provide all the meat for the allowances, which they cannot receive into the kitchen until after inspection by the *Prodomi*.

There are fourteen servants, called warders, two of whom, are set apart for the knights, *(persone dell' Abito)*. It is their duty to attend to the care of the sick day and night.

Besides these, there are two doorkeepers continually on guard to watch over the doors.

To assist the cooks and warders in the care of dirty vessels and other mean offices, about forty-four Christians and Turks are selected from the Prison of Slaves, for whom there is a separate Infirmary in the same prison.

Of the Ecclesiastics.

For looking after the spiritual welfare of the sick, the head is the Prior, who is a conventual *frère* chaplain, who has the charge of reconciling (to the Church) all the sick who come to the Hospital before twenty-four hours are over, in case they should not recover ; and he superintends the administration of the sacraments, and attends to the dying; and to take care of these latter, as well as the other cases, is his business by night and by day; and he confesses the sick.

Il Vice-Priore, che è nazionale Maltese per comodo della lingua amministra i sacramenti, conduce ivi morti nel cimitero contiguo al Infermeria, ascolta le confessioni, e assiste si di notte come di giorno alli moribondi, secondo il-giro, che li spetta, e suol'essere fra capellano d' ubbidienza.

Per ajuto di questi, due vi sono otto sacerdoti fra cappellani d'ubbidienza, due, dé quali destinati ad udire le confessioni, che in giro fanno indispensabilmente di giorno, e di notte le guardie, per la assistenza de' poveri moribondi, e a quelli, che non possono ajuvarsi danno caritativamente da mangiare con le proprie mani riscaldando a chi vuole le pitanze raffreddate.

Il Sagrestano oltre l'assistenza alle messe, e communione, avisa il priore, vice-priore, e sacerdoti per li sacramenti, e assistenza de malati gravi, e però nella visita segue il medico, per riferire quello, che si ordina.

Oltre di che si fa dalla Sacra Religione un'annua gratificazione al papas Greco, il quale viene dalla sua parrocchia per amministrare i sacramenti a quelli del suo rito, e nazione, che si ritrovano nella detta Sacra Infermeria, nella quale dalla Domenica in Albis fino ali Ascenzione, tutte le Domeniche il clero della conventual chiesa di San Giovanni, con apresso lo Eminentissimo Gran Maestro, Gran Croci, e Cavalieri si porta processionalmente, e nell' altare maggiore di essa doppo molte pie orazioni, si canta l'evangelio; Cum sederit Filius hominis, etc., e ció per eccitare i Cavalieri maggiorimente nell'opere della misericordia, e principalmente dell'ospitalità, che professano.

Delli Medici.

Li medici principali sono trè, i quali scambiano vicendevolmente ogni mese, e tiene cadauno di essi la sua abitazione nell' Infermeria al servizio della quale sono assidui visitandola tutta due volte il giorno, e ciò che da essi si ordina puntualmente si eseguisce; notando nelle tabelle affisse a cadaun letto il mangiare, e medicamenti.

Per ajuto di questi vi sono due altri medici prattici, i quali fanno anche un mese per uno, e hanno la stanza nell'Infermeria.

The Vice-Prior, who, for the convenience of the language, is a native of Malta, administers the sacraments, conducts the funerals in the cemetery adjoining the Infirmary, hears the confessions, and attends night and day to the dying, according to his turn; and he is subject to the frère chaplain. To assist these two there are eight priests owing obedience to the *frère* chaplains; two of these are set apart to hear the confessions, which they take it in turn to do by night and by day; they attend to the poor dying ones; and those who cannot feed themselves they charitably help with their food, warming up the portion that has got cold of any one that wishes it. The Sacristan, besides, assists them at the masses and communions, gives notice to the prior, vice-prior, and priests about the sacraments, and attends to the very grave cases; and therefore, at the hour of visiting, he follows next to the doctor to hear what has been prescribed.

Besides this, an annual gratuity is granted by the Holy Religion to a Greek pope, who comes from his parish to administer the sacraments to those of his persuasion and nationality, who are in the aforementioned Holy Infirmary; in which place, every Sunday, from Low Sunday *(Domenica in Albis)* to Ascension, the clergy of the conventual church of St John assemble in procession after the Most Eminent the Grand Master, Grand Crosses, and Knights, and at the high altar, after many pious orations, is sung the Gospel. "Cum sederit Filius hominis," &c.; especially to stir up the knights to deeds of mercy, and principally to the hospitality which they profess.

Of the Physicians.

There are three principal physicians who change about, each in his turn, every month, and reside in the Infirmary - attending to it most diligently, visiting it all over twice a-day, to see that their orders are punctually carried out, writing on the tablets attached to each bed the food and medicine required. To assist them there are two other experienced physicians, who take it also in turn every month, and have a room in the Infirmary.

Il prattico di mesata osserva più volte fra il giorno gli varj sintomi dell Infermi per riferirli al medico primario nella visitá; e a tal'effetto nonsimuta il pratico, che quindici giorni doppo essere entrato il medico, acciò quando viene il mese dell'altro sappia darli le dovute informazioni sopra lo stato de Malati. Assiste di più con l'Infirmiere e Priore nel tempo della mancia, facendo ritardare la pitanza a chi deve, e accudendo per tutto ció che potesse occorrere.

Tiene ivi oltre la Sacra Religione salariato un medico per la publica lettura quotidiana-di anatomia e accioche maggiormente si esercitino i principianti ogni Mercoledì si tiene publica accademia, nella quale si discorre sopra i morbi correnti.

Delli Chirurghi.

Li chirurghi primarj sono tré e questi si cambiano a vicenda, come i midici ogni mese, stanziando anche nell'Infermeria per curare i feriti d'ogni sorte, facendosi quivi perfettamente l'operazione del taglio della pietra, e la cura delle cataratte, perchè vi è continuo concorso de' forastieri, che vengono per ricuperare la salute.

A questi sono annessi nella istessa guisa due prattici, i quali hanno l'incombenza di far'eseguire ciò, che da' chirurghi si ordina, aiutando i medesimi nelle ore della visita, e accudendo nel tempo della mancia, come sopra, e hanno l'abitazione nell' Ospedale.

Vengono doppo questi sei giovani ajutanti, che si dicono barberotti, i quali dormono nell'Infermeria, e accudiscono alli chirurghi, ajutandoli in tutto ció, che sa di mestiere, e da questi si fanno scambievolmente le guardie per non lasciare senza la dovuta assistenza l'Infermi, e per riparare alli casi repentini.

Vi è di più un barbiere fisico che ha stanza nell'Infermeria, e hà la cura dell'insagnie, cataplasmi, vissicanti, ed altro spettante alla fisica, e tiene sotto la sua disciplina due giovani salariati.

Per curare la tigna si tiene una prattica donna attempata separatamente dall'Ospedale.

The doctor for the month notes several times a-day the symptoms of the sick, to relate them to the haed-physician at his visit; and to effect this, the doctor does not change until fourteen days after the physician has entered into residence, so that when it is the other doctor's turn, he may know what to tell him about the health of the sick. He also assists the Infirmarian and Priors at the time of the *mancia*, seeing that the proper persons receive the allowances and attending to anything that might occur.

The Holy Religion keeps, besides, a paid physician for the public daily lecture on anatomy; and in order, more especially, that the beginners may be trained, a public lecture is held every Wednesday, at which ordinary diseases are discussed.

Of the Surgeons.

There are three surgeons, and they take it in turn every month to attend, like the physicians, residing likewise in the Infirmary, having in charge the wounded of all sorts, performing here to perfection the operation of lithotomy, and the cure of cataract, for there is a continual concourse of strangers who come to recover their health.

To them are attached, in the same manner, two practitioners, who must see that the surgeons' orders are carried out, assisting them at the visitations, and at the *mancia;* and they live in the Hospital.

There are also six young men assistants called *barberotti*, who sleep in the Infirmary and assist the surgeons, helping them in everything concerning their profession; and they take it in turn to be on duty, so as not to leave the Infirmary without proper assistance, especially in sudden cases.

There is also a barber-surgeon or phlebotomist, who has a room in the Infirmary, and has charge of the leeches, cataplasms, *vissicanti*, &c., pertaining to medical things, and has under him two paid young men.

An experienced elderly woman is retained, apart from the hospital, to attend to cases of scurvy.

Della Speziaria.

L'officiali della speziarla sono un speziale primario, e cinque ajutanti salariati per la distribuzione delli medicamenti.

Dalli Prodomi si da' al speziale tutto il bisognovole per li restauranti, decotti, e brodi alterati, che si dispensano anche in gran quantità fuori dell'Infermeria a poveri, e povere, che ricorrono con supliche a piedi dell' Eminentissimo Gran Maestro, oltre ogni sorte di latte che da medici si ordini.

Dalla speziarla della Religione non solo si serve tutto l'Ospedale, e gl'officiali, ma ancora tutti luoghi pii, cioé:

Qualtro monasterj di monache che sono nella Valletta e Borgo.

Qualtro conservatorj di zitelle trà quali ve ne sono due, che si mantengono dall'Eminentissimo Gran Maestro, che con la sua pietà nè fondò uno.

Una casa di ripentite, che campa d'elemosina incerte.

Il convento de' P. P. Capuccini bastando la poliza del Guardiano.

Il convento de' P. P. Carmelitani Scalzi al Borgo, il quale hà il medico, e chirurgo salariato dalla Religione.

Equello de' P. P. Zoccolanti, i quali possono a libertà loro, come tutti gl'altri regolari venire a curarsi nell' Infermeria, nella quale sono con specialitá assistiti, siccome i religiosi di religione fuori di Malta che vengono per curarsi, come tutti i pellegrini, che hanno letto e pitanza, oltre li medicamenti a tutti i poveri e povere.

Delle Sale.

Si osserva nella Sacra Infermeria la dovuta separazione dei morbi, e condizione di malati, e però ad ogni sala è destinata la sua specie differente, cioè:

Sala per li cavalieri, e persone dell' Abito, ch' è la più commoda, e per gli feriti or sono assegnate due buone stanze.

Sala vecchia per le persone civili, e regolari, e pellegrini.

Sala grande per gli febricitanti, e altri morbi legieri.

Saletta per li gravi, e moribondi, con una camera contigua.

Of the Dispensary.

The officials of the Dispensary consist of a head-dispenser and five paid assistants for the distribution of medicines. The dispenser receives everything necessary from the *Prodomi* for restoratives, decoctions, and different soups, which are also dispensed in large quantities outside the Infirmary to poor people, who come with petitions to the Most Eminent the Grand Master; besides this, each one has milk who has been ordered it by the physicians.

The dispensary of the Religion not only provides for all the Hospital and for the officials, but also for all the religious places - i.e., four monasteries of nuns at Valetta and Borgo; four Homes for girls, two of which are supported by the Most Eminent the Grand Master, who of his piety has founded one; a penitentiary which is maintained by casual charity; the convent of P. P. Capuchins, an order from the Father Superior being sufficient; the convent of P. P. Carmelites Scalzi at Borgo, which has a paid physician and surgeon from the Religion; and that of the P. P. Franciscans, who can, if they wish, like all the other religious orders, come and be cured in the Infirmary, in which place they are especially attended to; as well as other religious orders outside Malta who come to be cured, and also all the pilgrims, who are given a bed and allowance, besides the medicines dispensed to all poor people.

Of the Wards.

The proper separation of the diseases and condition of the sick is observed in the Holy Infirmary, and therefore every room has its different use - *i.e.*:

Ward for the knights and persons of the Habit, which is most comfortable (convenient), and there are two good rooms set apart for the wounded.

An old ward for the laity, religious orders, and pilgrims.

Large ward for feverish and other slight ailments.

A small ward for serious cases and the dying, with a room adjoining.

Sala nuova per li flussanti, con due camere per quelli, che si tagliano la pietra.
Sala delli feriti con due camere.
Salane grande per le genti di catena, e due camere.
Stanza per li matti con suo guardiano.
Sale due per quelli dell'unzione mercuriale separate dalla Infermeria.
Una sala per quelli che pigliano le stuffe fuori dell'Infermeria per ovviare ogni sospetto di mal'aria, che potessero causare.
Ogni sala nell'Infermeria ha la sua Cappella ben' adorna per comodo della messa, e oltre queste vi è la Cappella del Santissimo Sacramento, che ha la porta verso la sala delli moribondi per comodo del viatico.
Il numero ordinario degli infermi è in circa 350 in 400 li quali si trattengono anche per tutta la loro convalescenza.

Delli Letti, Lenzuola, e Coperte.

Li letti degl'infermi sogliono di tempo in tempo mutarsi per la convenevole polizia, e si rifanno ogni sera dalli guardiani, che devono tenerli politi.
Li letti con padiglione, o cortinaggio sono in tutto trecento settanta, mutandosi l'estate con padiglioni di tela bianca, quelli senza padiglione sono trecento settanta cinque.
Quelli però usati da persone di morbo sospetto di etticia, o altro si bruciano con tutte le lenzuola ed altre spettanti robbe senza riserva alcuna.
I cavalieri e fratelli dell'Abito, hanno lenzuola separate, e più fine, li secolari anche si distinguono dalle genti di catena, massime i religiosi, e pelligrini, e in tutto ascendono al numero di mille cinque cento diecisette.
Le lenzuola si mutano senza riserva alcuna secondo il bisogno degl'infermi, ancorché bisognasse scambiarle moltissime volte tra il giorno.
Le coperte sono ancora distinte e separate come le lenzuola, essendovene per cavalier e religiosi, secolari e gente di catena, e sono in tutto mille cento e quattordici.

A new ward for those who suffer from hemorrhage, with two rooms for those who undergo lithotomy.
Ward for the wounded, with two rooms.
A very large ward for galley-slaves, and two rooms.
Room for mad people and their warder.
Two wards for those undergoing mercurial anointing, separate from the Infirmary.
A ward for those who take hot baths, outside the Infirmary, to avoid any idea of infection.
Every ward in the Infirmary has its chapel well fitted up for the convenience of Mass; and besides these, there is the Chapel of the Most Holy Sacrament, the door of which opens towards the ward for the dying, for the convenience of the viaticum.
The ordinary number of the sick is from about 350 to 400, who remain until they are convalescent.

Of the Beds, Sheets, and Coverlets.

The beds of the sick are changed from time to time for requisite cleanliness, and they are remade every evening by the warders, whose duty it is to keep them clean.
The beds with curtains number in all 370, which are changed in the summer for white linen curtains; those beds without curtains number 375.
Those beds used by persons suffering from consumption or other complaints are burnt, with all the sheets and other things belonging, without any reservation.
The knights and brothers of the Habit have separate sheets of a finer quality; the laity are also distinguished from the slaves, especially the monks and pilgrims; and, altogether, the number is 1517.
The sheets are changed, without exception, according to the needs of the sick, even though they should require changing several times a-day.
The coverlets, again, are distinct and separate like the sheets - being for the use of the knights and monks, seculars and galley-slaves, and number in all 1140.

Tanto le lenzuola, come le coperte, usate che siano, fino ad un certo segno si distribuiscono a' poveri, e povere mendicanti dalli Prodomi.

Dell'Argenteria.

Contribuisce molto al decoro della Sacra Infermeria, e polizia degl'infermi l'essere questi senati mattina, e sera con posate, scudelle, e tondini d'argento anzi l'estessi caldaroni, dalle quali si distribuiscono le minestre, e libacili grandi dove si tiene carne e altro sono d'argento come appare dalla seguente nota, alle gente di catena si supplisce con stagno: -

	Numero	Di peso lib.
Scodelle,	250	333.4
Piatti,	356	340.9
Piatti Grandi,	1	4.2
Tazze,	167	160.8
Bacili Grandi,	3	49.6
Bacilotti,	12	22.0
Cocchiere,	256	54.6
Cocchiaroni,	10	19.6
Forchette,	10	2.6
Quartucci,	43	36.1
Tazze a Becco,	4	4.0
Vasi a Becco,	1	1.0
Scatole,	1	1.0
Lampade,	13	59.1
Pignatte tra gradi, e piccoli con coperchio,	8	135.9
Bocali,	4	8.1
Soltocappa,	1	2.1

Argenti per la Cappella.

Candelieri,	6	34.9
Secchio e Asperserio,	1	4.6
Scatola per l'Ostia,	1	0.8
Calici con loro Patene,	5	
Pisidi Tré,	3	

The sheets as well as the coverlets, when old, are distributed after a certain time to poor beggars by the *Prodomi*.

Of the Silber Plate.

It contributes greatly to the dignity of the Infirmary and to the cleanliness of the sick, their being served night and morning with covers, bowls, and plates of silver; even the small boilers from which the soup is served, and the large dishes for holding meat, and other things, are of silver, as will appear from the following list. The slaves are supplied with pewter utensils: -

	Number	Weighing lb.
Bowls,	250	333.4
Dishes,	356	340.9
Large Dishes,	1	4.2
Cups,	167	160.8
Large Basins,	3	49.6
Basins,	12	22.0
Spoons,	256	54.6
Large Spoons,	10	19.6
Forks,	10	2.6
Quart-measures,	43	36.1
Drinking-cups,	4	4.0
Drinking-vessels,	1	1.0
Caskets,	1	1.0
Lamps,	13	59.1
Pots in sizes, and small ones with lids,	8	135.9
Jugs,	4	8.1
Salver,	1	2.1

Chapel Plate.

Candlesticks,	6	34.9
Bucket and holy-water Sprinkler	1	4.6
Casket for the Host,	1	0.8
Chalices with Patents,	5	
Three small Vases,	3	

Della Tapezzaria e Quadri.

L'inverno per maggior commoclo de malati si adornano le mura delle sale con arazzi di lana, i quali sono consegnati al linciere che ne ha cura, e questi sono divisi in cento trentuno pezzi.

L'estate poi restano adornate le sale con quadri, che sono con buona simitria dapertutto divisi rappresentando molti di essi l'istorie della Sacra Religione, e in tutto ascendono al numero di 85 compresi l'altari.

Della Qualita delle Pitanze.

Sopra di ogn'altra cosa s'invigila dalli Prodomi sopra la buona qualitá della robba, che suol servire per le pitanze, pigliando sempre la megliore, e perciò si danno all infermi ottimi consumati di galline, erbette, vermicelli, riso, e pisti, e tutte quelle sorti di carni, che li sono ordinate come di gallina, piccione, pollastro, vitella, vitellazza, caccia, piccatiglio frigassia stufato polpette, in quella quantitá, che conviene, oltre l'amendolate, ove fresche, prugna, e zibibo, e ogni sorte di rinfresco permesso a malati, come restauranti, biscotini, pomi, e granati con zuccaro e altre sorte di confetture; secondo il bisogno di caduno; alli cavalieri, e personne dell'Abito si dá pitanza doppia.

Camicie che Dispensano.

E'commendabile caritá quella, che si usa con i poveri, che vengono nell'Infermeria a curarsi tutti logori, e stracciati mentre non solo hanno il commodo di mutarsi la camicia, ma ancora gli se ne da una, guariti, che siano per carità e ogn'anno si dispensano in questa maniera cento sessanta camicie nuove.

Of the Hangings and Pictures.

For the greater comfort of the sick in winter, the walls of the rooms are hung with woollen curtains, which are given into the care of the *Linciere,* who has the charge of them, and there are 131 of them. In the summer time the rooms are ornamented with pictures, which are well hung all about - many of them representing the history of the Holy Religion; and in all they number 85, including the altar ones.

Of the Quality of the Food.

The *Prodomi,* above everything, look after the good quality of the materials used in the preparation of the food, selecting always the best of everything; and therefore the sick are given the best soups made of gallinas, herbs, vermicelli, rice, and minced meat, and every kind of meat which has been ordered them - such as gallinas, pigeons, fowls, beef, veal, game, hashes, fricassees, stews, forced meats - in such quantities as are necessary; besides milk of almonds, fresh eggs, plums and raisins, and every kind of refreshment allowed sick people - such as restoratives, sweet biscuits, apples and pomegranates with sugar, and other sorts of confectionery - according to the wants of each one. The knights and persons of the Habit receive double portions.

Of Shirts which are given away.

This is a commendable charity which the poor make use of who come to the Infirmary to be cured, all tattered and torn; for they not only enjoy the comfort of changing their shirts, but one is given to each of them for charity when they have recovered; and every year 160 new shirts are given away in this manner.

Dell'Assistenza de' Fratelli nella Sacra Infermeria.
Si esercità da' Fratelli dello Ordine Gerosolimitano la St. ospitalitá, e però nel tempo della mancia vengono a servire l'infermi con portare loro dal luogo dove si dispensa il mangiare sino alli letti le pitanze ordinatele, e quelle scambiano, permettendolo il medico assistente con altra cosa, se non gustassero a' medesimi infermi, a' quali i predetti Fratelli sogliono secondo riscaldare anche le pitanze, e prestarli tutta l'assistenza dovuta.

Ma perché venendo tutti insieme potrebbesi cagionar confusione perciò ciascheduna lingua ha la sua giornata assegnata per il servizio della Sacra Infermeria.

La Domenica per la lingua di Provenza.
Il Lunedi per quella di Alvernia.
Il Martedì per quella di Francia.
Il Mercoldi per quella d'Italia.
Il Giovedì per quella d'Aragona.
Il Venerdì per quella d'Alemagna.
Il Sabato per Castiglia e Portugallo.

Li Novizzi sono obligati di venire a servire nell'Infermeria come sopra, cioè ciascheduno nel giorno della sua lingua, ed acciocché non si manchi da alcuno ad un'opera di Caritá tanto dovuta, s'invigila dal maestro de' Novizj Gran Croce, e dalli due commissarj suoi colleghi di diversa nazione, che portano seco uno scrivano per notare chi di loro mancasse di venire per ammonirlo.

In oltre il Giovedì Santo il Gran Ospidaliere con tutti i cavalieri della lingua di Francia nella sala dove si fa il sepolcro con esemplar carità si portano a lavar i piedi a dodici poveri a quali poscia somministrano una buona elemosina.

Della Sepultura de' Morti nella Sacra Infermeria.
Li morti nell'Infermeria sogliono seppellirsi nel cimiterio della medesima; siccome quelli della casa detta la Falanga, e nell'oratorio di esso vi è la messa quotidiana per suffraggio de'medesimi defonti ivi seppelliti;

Of the Assistance of the Brethren in the Holy Infermeria.

The training of the Brothers of the Order of Jerusalem prescribes religions hospitality; and therefore at the time of the *mancia* they arrive to wait on the sick, and bring them to their beds, from the place where the food is dispensed, the portions ordered them, and these they exchange, if the physician on duty permits, for something else, if the sick do not fancy what is prepared for them; the aforementioned Brothers must also warm up the portions, and so give them all necessary assistance. But as all arriving together might cause confusion, each Langue has its own particular day assigned for the service of the Holy Infirmary.

Sunday, for the langue of Provence.
Monday, for that of Auvergne.
Tuesday, for that of France.
Wednesday, for that of Italy.
Thursday, for that of Arragon.
Friday, for that of Germany.
Saturday, for Castille and Portugal.

The Novices are obliged to come and assist in the Infirmary as above - *i.e.,* each one on the day of his Langue; and that none shall omit such a proper work of charity, a watch is kept by the master of the Novices, Grand Cross, and by two commissaries of the college, of different nationality, who bring with them a clerk to note the names of those who fail to come, so as to admonish them. Besides this, on Holy Thursday, the Grand Hospitaller, with all the knights of the French Langue, assemble in the room where the sepulchre is prepared, and with exemplary charity wash the feet of twelve poor men, to whom plentiful alms are given afterwards.

Of the Burial of the Dead in the Holy Infirmary.

The dead in the Infirmary are usually buried in its cemetery, as well as those of the house called La Falanga, and in its oratory there is daily mass said for the repose of the souls of the people buried there;

e se alcumo disponesse altrove la sua sepoltura in tal caso accompagnato il cadavere dal clero dell'Infermeria sino alla porta viene ivi consegnato alla parrocchia soggétta all' Oratorio.

Tutti quelli però, dell'Abito di tutti i stati sogliono seppellirsi nella conventual chiesa di San Giovanni, venendoli processionalmente a prendere il clero della medesima, e sei cavalieri per condurre il cadavere, se è cavaliere, o sei fra cappellani, se è fra cappellano, con il seguitto di Monsignor Prior della chiesa, Gran Croci, e convento.

Li donati, servitori, e famiglari de cavalieri volendosi seppellire fuori vengono associati dalla parrochia dell Vittoria della Religione.

Elemosine fisse estraordinarie che escono dalla Sacra Infermeria. Riassumendo l'Elemosine dell'Ospedale, queste sono considerabili per la qualitá, e quantità; primeramente, come già si è detto è cura dei Prodomi provedere di quotidiano assegnamento tutti i poveri ciechi, stroppi, leprosi, scrofolarj, ed altri invalidi, i quali presentemente importano scudi cento il mese.

Si distribuisce a' mendicanti, e invalidi consumato, e pasta mattina, e sera, e si dispensano senza reserva alcuna, legature, stampelle, e bastoni, e lenzuola, e coperte usate.

Si ricevono tutti i bambini esposti col provederli di Balie, alle quali si dá mesata, e vestiario, se li da stato nell' età più adultà, collocandosi ogn'anno in matrimonio sette zitelle orfane concinquanta scudi di dote per ciascheduna, altre si mettono in conservatorio, ed altre al servizio de' particolari: Oltre questi ve n' è un gran numero di poveri fanciulli, rimasti privi de' parenti, o per impossibilità de' medesemi al loro sostentamento, i quali sono soccorsi come gl'Esposti, e consegnati a suo tempo a chi spettano.

Alli P. P. Capuccini infermi si dà tanto di mangiare come di medicamenti tutto ciò, che li occorre, e á P. P. di S. Teresa al Borgo oltre; il commodo che si dà a tutti nell'Infermeria.

and if any one should wish to be buried somewhere else, the clergy of the Infirmary in such a case accompany the corpse to the place where it is to be buried, where it is consigned to the care of the parish priest, subject to the Oratory. All those, however, of the Habit, of every rank, are buried in the conventual church of St John - the clergy of the same arriving there in procession to receive them, and six knights to carry the corpse, if it be a knight, or six *frère* chaplains, if it be a *frère* chaplain - accompanied by the Monsignor Prior of the Church, Grand Crosses, and the convent fraternity. The donats, servants, and families of the knights wishing to be buried elsewhere, are accompanied by the parish priest of the Citta Vittoriosa.

The Ordinary and Extraordinary Charities of the Holy Infirmary.
Summing up the charities of the hospital, these will be found considerable for quality and quantity. In the first place, as has already been mentioned, it is the business of the *Prodomi* to provide daily allowances to all the poor blind, lame, leprous, scrofulous people, and other invalids, which amount at the present time to 100 *scudi* the month. Soup and vermicelli are distributed morning and night to the beggars and invalids; and bandages, crutches, sticks, linen, and old coverlets are given away to each one without reservation.

All deserted children are admitted and provided with nurses, who receive a monthly payment, and clothing if they are older, settling in marriage every year seven orphan girls, each one receiving 50 *scudi* dowry; others are placed in the *Conservatorio,* and others in the service of private persons. Besides these, there are a large number of poor children, left without relatives, or unable to be supported by them, who are assisted, like the foundlings, and sent back in time to those to whom they belong. To the sick of the P. P. Capuchins is given as much as they want in the way of food and medicines, and to the P. P. of St Theresa at Borgo, besides all the conveniences which all in the Infirmary receive.

Di più si allogiano tutti i Maroniti, Greci, e Pellegrini di Terrà Santa sino a nuovo imbarco.

A tutti i Missionarj Cappuccini, Teresiani, Zoccolanti, ed altri si da il soccorso di pane, e ova, e altro per il viaggia tanto nell'audare come nel venire dalla missione.

In oltre ogn' anno si dispensano scudi cinquanta à poveri di Bormola una delle 4 citta, dove maggiormente regna la povertà.

Enella settimana santa nella cena si dispensano diverse altre elemosine.

Calcolo della Speza annua che fa nell'Infermeria della
Sacra Religione

Attese tutte queste Elemosine, si fa il conto, che un Anno per l'altro la spesa totale della Sacra Infermeria solamente importi alla Religione scudi sessanta mila in circa.

Moreover, all the Maronites, Greeks, and pilgrims from the Holy Land are lodged until they embark again.

To all the missionary Capuchins, Theresians, and Franciscans, and others, bread and eggs are given, and also for the journey they receive as much on their return as on arrival.

Besides this, 50 *scudi* are given away every year to the poor of Burmola, one of the four towns where there is especially poverty; and in Holy Week, at the supper, various other charities are dispensed.

Calculation of the Annual Expenditure at the Infirmary
of the Holy Religion

Including all these charities, it is reckoned that from one year to another, the total expenditure of the Holy Infirmary alone, costs the Religion about 60,000 *scudi,*

REGOLAMENTO

PER

LE POVERE INFERME DI MALTA

Accioché le povere inferme esistenti nelle quattro città Valletta Borgo, Isola, e Bormola, e nell'Isola di Malta habiano il soccorso dovuto si nominano dall'Eminentissimo Gran Maestro due cavalieri proféssi di differente. Nazione, che si dicono commissarj delle povere inferme, i quali fanno un mese per uno, e hanno la cura di fare ogni principio di settimana una lista delle povere inferme che si trovano nelle quattro città per darle il convenevole mantenimento. Invigilano sopra i medici acciò facciano il lor dovere, visitando ogni giorno le povere scritte in lista, e scrivendo i medicamenti a chi inerita, e con la dovuta carità; per il quale effetto sogliono spesso visitare le suddette povere nelle loro case per sovenire a'bisogni di ogn'una, con soccorsi anche sopranumerarj, e per farli dare dalle pitanzerie la pietanza assegnatale, e sopra i chirurghi, acciò medichino tutte le prove ferite, di posteme, ed altro con la dovuta assistenza.

Li commissarj delle povere devono rivedere ad una per una tutte le polize de' medicamenti, scritte da'medici, e firmarle di proprio pugno, acciò siano dalla speziarla della Santa Religione servite.

Li medesimi provedono tutte le vacanze, che seguono per morte di povere, che avevano assegnamento ò di pane, ò di denari fissi ad altre meritevoli, e fanno le relazioni sopra le supliche che fanno le inferme all' Eminentissimo Gran Maestro.

REGULATIONS

FOR

THE SICK POOR OF MALTA

In order that the sick poor living in the four towns, Valletta, Borgo, Isola, and Burmola, and in the island of Malta, should receive proper assistance, two professed knights of different nationality are nominated by the Most Eminent the Grand Master, who are called Commissioners of the sick poor. They take it in turns by the month, and are intrusted with making a list, at the beginning of each week, of the sick poor in the four towns, in order to give them the proper assistance. They superintend the doctors, to see they perform their duty and visit each day the poor whose names are down on the list, noting the remedies for those who require, them, with due charity. To effect this, they are accustomed frequently to visit the above-mentioned poor at their homes, to relieve the wants of each, with the assistance of supernumeraries, and to see that they are given the portions allowed them from the *Pitanziera,* and also that the surgeons attend to the abscesses, wounds, &c. properly.

The commissioners of the poor must examine one by one the prescriptions written by the doctors, and sign them with their own hand, that they may be given out from the dispensary of the Holy Religion.

They take care that the vacancies which occur by the death of the poor who are receiving an allowance of either food or money, are filled up by other deserving cases, and inform the Most Eminent the Grand Master of the petitions made by the sick.

Usano tutte le calitele acciò le povere che si soccorrono siano di buona vita, secondo le loro lodevoli ordinazioni, ed a tale effetto tutte le polize della campagna, devono essere accompagnate con là fede del paroco, circa la povertà, e buona vità dell'inferme.

Li commissarj hanno un scrivano il quale nota tutta la spesa, che si fà tutto il pane, e dà esecuzióne a pagamenti per via di polize dalli medesimi firmate.

Vi sono inoltre quattro donne attempate, che si dicono pitanziere per le quattro città già dette, le quali hanno il carico di consegnare giorno per giorno alle. Povere inferme il soccorso assegnatoli da commissarj, dovendo ogni settimana portare ai medesimi le liste che saranno tutte da'medici, per prendere gl'ordini oportuni.

Di più devono accompagnare i commissarj ogni qual volta questi vogliono, nelle visite che fanno per mostrarli le case delle povere inferme. Queste hanno quattro altre donne salariate per carreggiare il pane ogni giorno.

Delli Medici, e Chirurghi.

Li Medici sono cinque, cioè: -
Due per la Città Valletta.
Uno per il Borgo.
Uno per l'Isola.
Uno per Bormola.

E questi salariati espressamente dalla Religione per servizio delle povere e sono obbligati di servire gratis a tutte le povere inferme li medicamenti necessarj, esprassando nelle polize il nome cognome, città e strada dell'inferma per renderne informato il commissario, avendo proibizione di scrivere a donne pubblice che devono andare all' Incurabile.

Fanno ogni settimana le liste di quelle, che meritano pitanza per essere esaminate dal commissario. Devono visitare gratis tutte le povere febricitante, e bisognose, e accompagnare il commissario quando fa le visite, essendo chiamati.

Li chirurghi sono ancora cinque, come i medici, e distribuiti nell' istessa maniera, e questi si regolano come i medesimi.

They take every precaution that the poor who apply for relief are leading a respectable life, according to their praiseworthy regulations; and to effect this, all the cases from the country must be accompanied by the recommendation of the parish priest as to the poverty and respectability of the sick.

The commissioners have a clerk, who notes all expenses, all the bread consumed, and sees that payment is given by means of tickets signed by them.

There are, moreover, four elderly women who are called *Pitanziere,* for the four towns already mentioned, who are charged with dispensing, day by day, to the sick poor the succour accorded them by the commissioners, and every week they must bring them the lists, which shall be all a physician's, to take the necessary orders.

Moreover they must accompany the commissioners every time the latter may desire it, in their visits, to show them the homes of the sick poor. These women have under them four other paid women, to carry about the bread every day.

Of the Physicians and Surgeons.

There are five physicians - *i.e.:* -
    Two for the city of Valetta.
    One for Borgo.
    One for Isola.
    One for Burmola.

And these are paid expressly by the Holy Religion for the service of the poor, and they are obliged to give out free the necessary medicines to the sick poor, declaring in the tickets the name, surname, town, and street of the sick person, for the information of the commissioners - being forbidden to register *donne pubblice,* who ought to go to the Incurable Home.

Every week they make a list of those who deserve an allowance, to be examined by the commissioner. They must visit free all the feverish and needy poor, and accompany the commissioner when required, when he makes his visits.

There also five surgeons, like the physicians, distributed in the same manner, and paid just the same.

Della Distibutione de' Medicamenti.

La persona, che vuole essere servita gratis di medicamenti dalla speziaria della Sacra Religione deve sopra tutto essere povera ed onorata, a tutte quelle, che hanno queste condizioni si dispensano per polize riviste da'commissarj dandoseli anche ogni sorte di brodi alterati, decotti, e latte secondo il bisogno.

Si dispensano anche a molte povere famiglie vergognose, mediante decreto, e a tutte quelle degl'officiali, come medici chirurghi, pitanziere, ed altri.

Soccorso che si d'alle Povere Inferme, che si dice Pitanza.

Fra il numero grande delle povere, che sono nella città, la maggior parte cascando inferme non possono con il semplice ajuto de' mendicanti, e medico pagato supplire alli bisogni della malattia, e perció dalli commissari vengono soccorse con quotidiane elemosine in tutto il tempo dell'infermità, dandoli alle più gravi un tari, e alle meno gravi un carlino, con il pane, riserbandosi a'commissarj di accrescersi secondo il bisogno quel tanto che giudicheranno; alle povere stroppie, e con malattie abituali si danno due tari la seltimana, e il pane giornale, sino a tanto che siano di qualche fissa elemosina proviste.

Tanto all'inferme in pitanza come ad altre si suole dalla cucina della Sacra Infermeria somministrare del consumato, e vermicelli per mezzo di polize de commissarj, come anche delle lenzuola, e coperte, per soccorrere alle necessita di ogni una.

Del Pane fisso, e estraordinario.

Si assegna dalla Sacra Religione una ragione di pane quotidiana alle povere invalide, e questa per tutta la loro vita. Il numero di queste presentemente, è di cento cinquanta, che importano altretanti

Of the Distribution of Medicines.

The person who wishes to be served free with medicine from the dispensary of the Holy Religion must be, above everything, poor and respectable. All those thus qualified receive what they require by tickets, revised by the commissioners, allowing them all kinds of different soups, boiled decoctions, and milk, according to their needs.

Medicines are also dispensed to many poor respectable families by means of an order, and to all those of the officials, such as physicians, surgeons, *pitanziere,* &c.

The Hole which is given to the Sick Poor, called Pitanza.

Among the large number of poor people who live in the town, the greater portion who fall ill cannot supply the needs of their illness with medicines and advice gratis alone, and therefore they are relieved by the commissioners with daily alms during the time of their illness, the most serious cases receiving a *tari* (three halfpence) and a couple of loaves of bread a-day, and the less serious a *carlino* (three farthings) and bread, the commissioners reserving to themselves the right, as they think fit, of increasing it; to poor cripples and to chronic cases are given two *tari* each week, and bread daily, unless they are in receipt of some regular charity.

To the sick, as well as to others, are given away allowances of soup and vermicelli from the kitchen of the Holy Infirmary, by means of tickets from the commissioners, as well as sheets and coverlets, according to the need of each one.

Of the Ordinary and Extraordinary Bread Allowances.

A ration of bread is allowed by the Holy Religion daily to all the poor invalids, and this for their lifetime. These number, at the present time, 150, which means twice as many loaves a-day,

paja di pane il giorno, oltre quelle, che sono in pitanza, le quali sono ordinariamente cento in tutte le città che come si disse hanno il pane, oltre il tari, o carlino, e quelle dissutili, le quali ascendone al numero di 50 in circa, benchè queste si scambiano a vicenda ogni settimana.

Mesate fisse.

Ogni principio di mese si fà dalli commissarj la paga, delle pitanze, o siano mesate fisse delle povere, le quali hanno morbi incurabili, e però si dicono dissutili, dandosi a ciascheduna più, o meno, secondo il bisogno e assegnamento, e queste arrivano alla somma di sessanta in settanta scudi il mese per le quattro città.

Della Casetta, o incurabile delle Donne.

Vi è nella Valletta una casa della la Casetta, o sia Incurábile delle povere donne, la quale non hà di rendita che quel poco li da una tenue fondazione, l'amministrazione della quale è raccomandata al cavaliere più anziano, che risieda in Malta della nazione Sanese; ma questa non potrebbe sostenere, che pochissimi letti, se non fusse in tutto soccorsa dalla Sacra Religione, la quale benchè non habbia in quel luogo giurisdizione spirituale, essendo assegnato alla, giurisdizione dell'ordinario si contenta però a solo titolo di carità di supplire a tutto il bisognevole per il suo commodo mantenimento; mentre non solo è di gran sollievo per le povere delle città ma aucora per quelle di tutta l'Isola, come si vedrà in appresso e per altre che non hanno ne tetto ne parenti per assistere.

Officiali.

Ordina per tanto la Sacra Religione alli predetti commissarj delle povere che habiano cura di quel luogo regolandolo nella forma megliore, e però da essi provedonsi le inferme di tutto il necessario

besides those who receive an allowance, who number usually 100 in all the towns, and who receive, as has been said, bread, besides a *tari* or a *carlino;* and those, disabled, who number about 50, although they vary in number every week.

Fixed Monthly Payments.

At the beginning of each month payments are made by the commissioners of allowances, or fixed monthly money, to the poor who suffer from incurable diseases, and are therefore denominated helpless, giving to each one more or less according to his need and position, and this sum averages from 60 to 70 *scudi* the month for the four towns.

Of the "Casetta" or Incurable Home for Women.

There is in Valletta a house called the "Casetta", or Incurable Home for Poor Women, which has no revenue, except that derived from a small endowment, the administration of which is committed to the charge of the senior knight, a native of Siena, residing in Malta; but this Home could only support a few beds if it were not assisted by the Holy Religion, who, although it has not any jurisdiction in that place, it being assigned to the jurisdiction of the ordinary, is content for charity's sake to supply everything that is necessary for its proper maintenance; whilst it is not only a great boon to the poor in the towns, but also to all those in the island, as will be seen hereafter, and for others who have neither home nor relatives to assist them.

Officials.

It is arranged, however, by the Holy Religion, that the abovementioned commissioners of the poor should look after that place, conducting it in the best manner, and taking care that the sick have

per la mancia invigilando sopra la buona qualità delia robba, e sopra la dovuta polizia delle sale, e servizio delle medesime.

Il commissario assiste le mattine nel tempo che si dispensa il mangiare, e la sera, e non potendovi andare lasciano l'incombenza al loro scrivano. Provede di letto tutte le povere inferme, senza però le loro polize non si riceve alcuna.

Vi è uno scrivano il quale fà li conti di tutta la spesa, e suol essere lo stesso de poveri.

Un'altro per andare a notare nella lista il mangiare scritto dai medici per provedere in tempo il necessario andando mattina, e sera a far dispensare il mangiare acciò ogni letto habbia la pitanza assegnatali, dando del tutto parte al commissario, se non vi sarà intervento.

Siegue un spezialotto che deve andare ogni mattina a buon ora a portare medicamenti alle inferme per fare, che ciascuna pigli quello, si sarà ordinato, senza confusione, e nell'ora della mancia interviene per scrivere li medicamenti nel suo libro, e notare tutto ciò che occorre nelle tavolette affisse a cadaun letto.

Mantiene di più la Sacra Religione nel detto Incurabile una donna, che si chiama Governatrice, la quale habita ivi, e hà in consegna tutta la biancheria esistente in lenzuole, coperte, cuscini, e matarazzi, che fornisce la sudetta fondazione; onde hà l'incombenza di dare letto a quelle che vengono con la poliza del commissario, secondo la loro condizione, e infermità inviglia che non entri a visitare le inferme che persona conosciuta, e fá serrare, e aprire alle ore dovute la porta, e accudisce sopra tutto alla polizia, e quiete dell'inferme.

Vi sono quattro serve salariate per servire le povere, facendosi da esse i letti, e tutto ciò, che spetta alla servitù dovutale.

Di più un' altra donna per ministrare la mancia, e riscaldare tutto ciò che fà di bisogno, e hà la cura di conservare sempre pronto del buon consumato per tutto ciò, che potesse occorrere in qualsivoglia tempo.

Si trattiene ancora un' homo il quale serve per 1 unzione mercuriale, e per carregiare ciò che fà di bisogno nell'incurabile.

Il mangiare si cocina nella Sacra Infermeria dove espressamente si paga il coco, e da quella si trasporta mattina, e sera nella casetta non molto distante da due schiavi à ciò destináti.

everything necessary by means of the *mancia* - inspecting the good quality of the food, and the proper cleanliness and service of the wards.

The commissioner attends in the morning when the food is dispensed, and in the evening; and if not able to be present, he leaves his clerk in charge.

He provides all the poor sick with beds; without tickets, however, none are received. There is a clerk who notes all expenses, and takes count of the poor.

Another notes in the list the food prescribed by the physicians, to provide in time what is necessary, going morning and evening to have the food dispensed, so that every bed may receive the allowance assigned it, keeping the commissioner informed about everything, if he is not present.

There is a dispenser also, who must attend early every morning to bring the medicines to the sick, to see that each one receives what has been ordered for him; and, at the time of the *mancia,* he attends, to write down the medicines in his book; and to note down everything that may occur on the tablets fixed to each bed.

The Holy Religion also maintains in the said Incurable Home a woman, who is called Governor, who lives there, and has in charge all the linen - consisting of sheets, coverlets, pillows, and mattresses - which the above-mentioned endowment provides. She has also the charge of giving beds to those who come with a ticket from the commissioner, according to their condition and ailment. She takes care that no one is allowed to visit but people who are known, and sees that the gate is shut and opened at the proper times, and, above all, looks after the cleanliness and repose of the sick.

There are four paid maid-servants to wait on the poor people, who make the beds, and do anything else necessary.

There is also another woman to serve out the *mancia*, and warm up anything that is wanted; and she has always to keep in readiness some good soup for anyone who may need it at any time.

A man is also retained for mercurial anointing, and to fetch and carry, as may be required.

The food is cooked in the Holy Infirmary, where a cook is expressly paid, and it is brought morning and evening to the "Casetta", which is not far distant, by two slaves kept for that purpose.

Per l'assistenza a Miribonde.

Ló spirituale benchè non appartenga alla Sacra Religione con tutto ciò essendoli sommamente a cuore l'assistenza delle povere inferme tiene a sue spese un sacerdote, per li moribondi e per le confessioni, il quale ha 'stanza, e letto nel detto luogo.
La matina con il commodo della messa hanno ancora quello del SS. Viatico, la sera però si porta dalla parrocchia di S. Paolo.
Le povere che ivi muojuono vengono a prendersi dalla confraternità della carità, nella quale sogliono ascriversi divoti Cavalieri, Gran Croci, e l'istesso Monsignor Vescovo, che spinto dalla sua carità spesso suole accompagnarle, e fare per l'anime di quelle molti Suffragj.

Delli Medici, Chirurghi, e Medicamenti.

Li medici, dell'Incurabile sono due siccome li chirurghi, e scambiano a vicenda ogni mese, solendo essere quelle delle povere Inferme di fuori, come si disse.
Il medico deve mattina e sera fare la visita di tutte le sale, come nella Infermeria si costuma ordinando ciò, che con viene. A quelle che si vogliono far curare fà la poliza dell'infirmità, la quale deve essere sottoscritta dal commissario, e ciò che fà il medico, deve anche il chirurgo nella suo professione dandosi di tutto parte al commissario.
Li medicamenti si scrivono dallo spezialotto nel libro che deve passare sotto l'occhio del commissario per firmarlo, e oltre li medesimi ordinarj si danno le sorti dé decotti, brodi alterati, e latte, e per tutti gl' officiali del detto luogo, secondo il bisogno.

Della Qualita delle Pitanze.

S'invigila dalli commissarj sopra la buona qualità delle pitanze, e perciò è loro inspezzione próvedere il tutto in quella forma che giudicano.

About Assistance for the Dying.

Although the spiritual assistance does not belong to the Holy Religion, still it is so much interested about the welfare of the sick poor, that it maintains at its own expense a priest to attend to the dying, and to confess, who has a room and bed in the place.

In the morning, besides mass, they have the most holy viaticum; in the evening it is brought from the parish church of St Paul, as well as extreme unction. The poor who die there are taken away by the confraternity of the charity - in whose ranks are included the names of devout Knights, Grand Crosses, and my Lord the Bishop himself, who, inspired by charitable feelings, often accompanies them, and says prayers for the repose of their souls.

Of the Physicians, Surgeons, and Medicines.

The physicians of the Incurable Home, as well as the surgeons, are two in number, and take it in turn every month to attend to the sick poor outside, as has been said. The physician must visit the wards morning and evening, as is the custom in the Infirmary, prescribing what is necessary. To those who want to be cured, he gives a voucher of illness, which must be undersigned by the commissioner, and the surgeon must do in his profession as the physician - informing the commissioner of everything.

The medicines are written down by the dispenser in a book, which must be shown to the commissioner to sign it; and, besides the usual medicines, different kinds of soups, boiled decoctions, and milk are dispensed, and by all the officials of the place, as may be needed.

Of the Quality of the Allowances.

The commissioners look after the good quality of the food, and therefore it is their duty to provide everything as they think fit.

Il consummato suol essere l'istesso, che si da all'infermi nella Sacra Infermeria.
La minestra quasi ogni giorno si muta faccendosi di zuppa, erbette, guiocchetti tagliolini, riso e altro.
La carne è di gallina, piccione pollastro, vitella, e vitellazza in polpette stufatto, o frigassia oltre li pisti caccia, amendolata biscottini, restauranti, e altre confetture permisse secondo il bisogno delle inferme alle quali si dà ogni sorte di cibo in caso d'inapetenza.

Numero delle Sale.

La sala nuova per quelle che pigliano decotti, brodi alterati, e latte.
   Sala vecchia per le febricitanti.
   Sala, delli spalmanti per l'unzione mercuriale.
   Sale, delle ferite per la chirurgia.
   Sala per le vecchie, e invalide.
   Camere due per le pazze.
   Camera per le parturienti.
A due di queste sale, cioè alla nuova, e vecchia vi è il suo altare.
Il numero ordinario delli letti suol essere di sessanta in settanta non compreso il tempo dell'unzione mercuriale.

Dell' Anzione Mercuriale, e Stufe.

Nella primavera, e principio d'autunno si dà la detta unzione senza riserva a chiunque povera ne habbia di bisogno nell'Incurabile; come anche le stufe, le quali per altro si danno in luogo separato, pagandosi a tal'effetto un stufatolo.

Delle Esposte e Dissutili.

Le povere esposte, che si nodriscono dalla Sacra Religione nella Falanga, cascando inferme si conducono nell'Incurabile dove sono

The broth is usually the same as that which is given to the sick in the Holy Infirmary. The soup varies almost every day, being made of soaked bread, herbs, *guiocchetti* (small plates of paste), vermicelli, rice, &c.

The meat consists of gallinas, pigeons, fowls, veal, and stewed forcemeat veal, and fricassees, besides game, almond-paste, fancy biscuits, restoratives, and other confectionaries - dispensed according to the needs of the sick, to whom is given every kind of food in case of want of appetite.

Number of Wards.

New ward for those who take boiled decoctions, different soups, and milk.

Old ward for fever cases.
Ward of anointers, for mercurial anointing.
Ward of the wounded for surgery.
Ward for the old and infirm.
Two rooms for the insane.
Room for lying-in.

Two of these wards, the new and old, have their altars.
The ordinary number of beds is from 60 to 70, not including the time of mercurial anointing.

Of Mercurial Anointing and hot baths.

In spring and the beginning of autumn the said anointing is given without reservation to any poor person in the Incurable Home who may stand in need of it, and also hot baths, which are given in a separate place. A man is paid to attend to these.

Of the foundlings and disabled.

The poor foundlings who are brought up by the Holy Religion in the Falanga, falling ill, are taken to the Incurable Home, where

con parzialità assistite dandoseli pitanza doppia, e letto migliore facendo la Religione con esse le parti di una pietosa madre.

Si ricevono ivi oltre nel detto luogo buon numero di povere vecchie, le quali per tutta la lor vita hanno un'assistenza grande ivi tutto ciò che li occorre; e ancora molte altre povere, le quali non avendo casa si tratengono a titolo di crità nell'Incurabile.

Tutta la minestra, che suol rimanere si dispensa a diverse povere, che ivi accorano, alle quali suol darsi anche una pagnotta.

> Somma del denaro che si dispensa dalli
> Commissarj delle Povere.

Attese tutte queste elemosine non contando il costo delli medicamenti, che può ognuno comprendere, dal dispensarne che si fà à tutte le provere dell'Isola di Malta e Gozzo; ne tampoco il pane che si dà a quasi tutte le inferme, e dissutili, e il salario de'medici, chirurghi e barbieri, il denaro, che si dispensa da' commissarj delle povere ascende in circa alta somma di tremila e nove cento scudi di rame. Sc. 3900.

they receive double allowances, and better beds, the Religion performing the part of a pitiful mother to them.

A large number of poor old people are received into the said place, who receive for all their lifetime every assistance in anything that may happen; and also many other poor persons, not possessing a home, are maintained by charity in the Incurable Home.

All the soup which remains over, is given away to various poor people who come there, who receive also a small loaf.

Amount of money which is given away by the Commissioners of the Poor.

Taking into account all these charities - not counting the cost of medicines, which any one may comprehend, from what is dispensed to all the poor in the island of Malta and Gozzo, nor the bread which is given to almost every sick person and disabled, and the salary of the physicians, surgeons, and barbers, - the money which is given away by the commissioners of the poor amounts to about 3900 *scudi* in money.

THE HOSPITAL OF THE KNIGHTS OF MALTA

VALETTA

SECTIONS OF PART OF THE HOSPITAL WARD

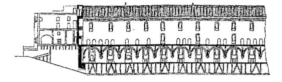

—LONGITUDINAL LOOKING WEST—   —TRANSVERSE—

REFERENCE TO DATES

—PART BUILT—
A.D. 1579
A.D. 1712
A.D. 1730

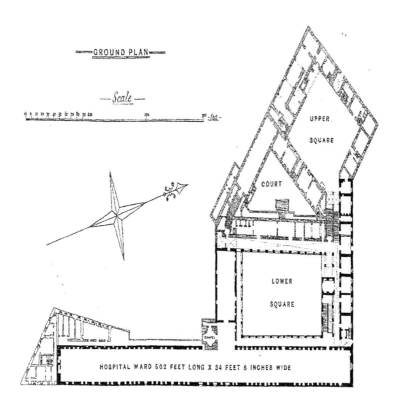

NOTES

NOTE A.

Paciaudius, in his work "De cultu S. Johannis Baptistae" (Rome, 1755), says, at Florence, *in commenda S. Jacobi in campo Corbellini*, which is opposite to the chapel and altar of St Mary de Lilliis, this inscription is carved in those characters which are vulgarly called Gothic: "In nome di dio amen, MCCCCLI. adi XIII di maggio questa capella si chiama la capella di sancta maria del giglio e del beato messer sancto giovanni - la quale hanno fatto i poveri attrati di mani e di piedi ed altra buona gente che e entrata con loro in eampagnia." He proceeds to give his opinion that this disorder, which attacked hands and feet, was epilepsy - known among the French in the fourteenth century as the *morbus Sancti Johannis*. The reason for the name, Paciaudius states, was this: At Creteil, about two leagues from Paris, there existed a very famous church, supposed to contain the graves of certain martyrs, put to death in the reign of Claudius Caesar, which were famed for miraculous cures. Yet the feast of St John Baptist surpassed in popularity those of the local saints, and epileptic patients especially resorted thither on that particular day; so that from the cures thus effected the disease itself became commonly known as St John's, - in fact, in 1737 the canons of the Church were forbidden, to keep up the nocturnal services, which had been abused by disorderly persons. It is supposed that from the fame of these miraculous events the term "il male di San Giovanni" took its rise; and that the "poveri attrati di mani et di piede" were patients whose flexor muscles and nerves were so distorted, contracted, and stiffened, as to cause deformity and wasting of the limbs; at any rate, it seems to have been an infliction so much akin to epilepsy as to suggest the intercession of the saint who was deemed to exercise the power of healing such an ailment.

That Christians wore the images of saints as intercessors against special complaints is well known. Paciaudius gives an engraving of a gem from the museum of Pope Benedict XIV., beautifully incised with a figure of St John Baptist, surrounded by a golden coronet, and with a shoe-latchet above, which he assumes to have been worn round the neck of an epileptic patient.

NOTE B

A picture in monochrome, in the chapel of the monastery of St Scolastiea, in the city Vittoriosa -which formed part of the first hospital erected by the knights of St John shortly after their arrival in the island - represents our Saviour armed with darts and surrounded by angels, with the Virgin praying as inscribed, *Fili miserere,* on the one side, and St John with inscription *Christe miserere* on the other. A little above, and in profile, are the two prophets - Elias and Enoch - in the act of adoration; the five figures forming a semicircular group in the cinquecento style: the background is powdered with fleurs-de-lys. On the lower part are two coats of arms, unknown - one a horse and a star, the other a chevron, between three birds. By one of these coats is the date 1557, marking the period of the picture.

The architecture of the chapel itself is Lombard, and remarkable for its elegance. Each capital is of distinct design, and at the top of each column are cherubs' heads, whose winged necks, interlaced, form a frieze. On the principal arch is a circle surrounded with rays, within which, in bas-relief, are the letters I.H.S. in antique character - the upper limb of the H traversed crosswise, illustrating the motto of Constantine, *In hoc signo vinces.* The date 1533, and the arms of Delisle Adam cut in stone, mark the epoch at which the chapel was erected; and the arches which support the hall and gate of the monastery are of similar architecture. The whole building, we may conjecture, was erected in this style, though now modernised.

NOTE C

Report of the Barrack and Hospital Commission, 1863

General Hospital, Valletta

This hospital is one of the most complicated buildings we have seen, and one of the most ill-arranged and unsuitable places for the sick of a garrison in existence.//
It is situated on the south-east side of Valletta, close to the great harbour, from which it is separated by a narrow public road and wall. The site is the lowest on that side of the town, and all the ground falls towards it.//
There is an apparent advantage of position derived from the proximity of part of the sick wards to the sea; but in a climate like that of Malta, where sanitary condition depends so much on the nature of the winds, this advantage is neutralised and converted into a disadvantage by the circumstance that all healthy winds are cut off from the building, partly by its bad construction, partly by its being enclosed on three sides by a densely packed neighbourhood of lofty houses, and also because the lofty works of Fort St Elmo intervene between the site of the hospital and the north and north-westerly winds, which are the really healthy winds. The only wind that blows directly on the sick wards is the sirocco, a well-known cause of indisposition at Malta, and the effect of which is immediately perceived on the sick. The site is hence exposed only to unhealthy winds; and at all other times there is more or less stagnation of air about it, unless there is stormy weather.//
Nothing in the construction tends to redeem this defect of position, but on the contrary; for the construction is bad in two essential matters: first, it consists of two courts, one of them 34 feet below the level of the other; secondly, both courts are closed at the angles; a form of construction which renders external ventilation very difficult at any time; and the lower court - that from which the ventilation along one side of a number of the sick wards is derived - is a

sunk area or well about 50 feet deep, measured from the roofs of the surrounding buildings.

There is no free circulation of air through this court, except such as comes over the tops of the buildings. It is the only place where convalescents can take exercise. It was being improved in appearance, by having a few trees and shrubs planted in it, while we were there; a praiseworthy attempt to render the place more cheerful, but very likely, if the trees should grow up, to impede still farther the ventilation, and render the air more damp.

The following is the general arrangement of the hospital buildings: The principal entrance is at the bottom of the steep slope of the Strada Mercanti. It is through an arch leading into a square paved court, enclosed by buildings two floors in height, containing officers' quarters, offices, pharmacy, apothecaries' stores, guard-room, &c. The upper floor on one side is occupied by sick wards. At the north-eastern corner of this square there is a large arched doorway, with a spacious flight of some twenty stone steps, enclosed in the buildings. The lower court, which is closed, and of a square form, is seen by looking over the corridor. One side of this court is cut out of the solid rock, the face of which is covered with patches of green vegetation, marking the presence of damp, and also of malaria in a warm climate. The other sides are principally formed by the hospital.

On the side next the upper square the corridor gives entrance to a number of dark, damp rooms - some of little or no use, except to harbour foul air or dirt. One of these, at the end furthest from the entrance, was being filled up as a bath or ablution room; perhaps the best available place for such accommodation, but nevertheless not a place where sick men or convalescents ought either to wash or bathe. The baths used formally to be in the upper square, quite away from the sick. Opposite the door of this bath-room are the hospital privies, which were most offensive, and diffused their odour right and left along the open corridor. The opposite side of the square is bounded by a long lofty building two floors in height.

117

The lower floor, opening from the ground-level of the lower court, is below the level of the ground outside, and contains stores of various kinds, the kitchen, disused stables, the dead-house, ablution room, &c. The upper floor is entered from the corridor, and contains one long, lofty ward. The other two sides of the square are occupied mainly by sick, but partly also by stores and non-commissioned officers' quarters. This is, however, not the whole of the accommodation for the sick. The long ward fronting the sea occupies only half the length of the hospital on that side. The building is prolonged to the south-east in the same front, and contains another long ward, facing the sea on one side, and almost blocked up along the opposite face by a line of stores built up against it, and by the narrow populous streets that environ it.

A very important disadvantage attending the length and position of the buildings is, that one of the main town sewers, draining a considerable district, passes directly under the middle of the hospital, while other two of the town sewers pass, one at either end. These sewers all open above water-mark, and give rise to most offensive odours during certain states of the weather. The lower floor of this part of the building is charged with foul air throughout, and at some parts it is scarcely safe to remain in the places for any length of time. The buildings were formerly the ho*spitium* of the knights; they are very old, and are supposed to have been amongst the earliest erected outside St Elmo. The following table gives the ward accommodation.

 Date of construction, A.D. 1575.
 number of wards, 20.
 Regulation number of beds, 382.

Wards	Regulation Number of Feet per Ward	Dimensions						Cubic Feet per Bed.	Superficial Feet per Bed.
		Length		Breadth		Height		Cubic Contents	
		ft.	in.	ft.	in.	ft.	in.	ft.	
13[11]	8	21	0	17	7	16	0	5,904	738	46
14	7	20	0	17	6	16	0	5,600	800	50
17	42	96	0	30	0	23	4	67,200	1600	68
18	4	30	6	17	0	15	4	7,950	1987	129
19	3	23	4	17	0	15	4	7,536	2512	132
22	9	50	0	18	6	13	8	12,641	1404	102
39	26	98	4	29	7	30	6	88,724	3412	111
40	7	26	0	17	6	17	4	7,886	1126	65
41	7	37	0	17	6	17	4	11,214	1602	92
42	5	29	0	17	6	17	4	8,788	1757	101
50	34	90	8	22	11	25	8	53,309	1567	61
52	6	34	6	19	2	16	8	11,016	1836	110
56	13	49	7	31	0	13	4	20,493	1576	118
57	11	21	0	21	4	19	8	8,810	300	40
58	13	59	0	18	6	19	5	21,183	1629	83
A 58	5	23	0	19	9	19	6	8,853	1770	90
60	14	42	8	34	10	30	6	45,323	3237	106
A 60	22	73	0	34	10	30	6	77,531	3524	115
B 60	34	110	0	34	10	30	6	116,843	3436	112
C 60	110	275	0	34	10	30	6	292,159	2655	87

---

[11] A small closet containing two beds, opening of No. 13, is not included. 13 and 14 are prisoners' wards.

Wards	Regulation Number of Feet per Ward	Windows		
		Number	Average Height	Average Width
			ft. in.	ft. in
13[12]	8	2	6 0	2 7
14	7	1	6 0	2 7
17	42	13{ 6 / 7	7 5 / 1 5	3 8 / 3 0
18	4	3	3 3	3 7
19	3	2	3 3	3 7
22	9	4	6 0	3 5
39	26	8	5 7	3 0
40	7	4	5 10	2 11
41	7	4	5 11	2 11
42	5	3	5 2	2 11
50	34	7{ 5 / 2	6 9 / 3 6	3 4 / 3 3
52	6	3	6 4	3 7
56	13			
57	11	6{ 5 / 1	5 3 / 2 8	4 4 / 1 8
58	13	2	7 2	3 3
A 58	5	6{ 5 / 1	6 8 / 3 0	3 10 / 1 8
60	14	2	6 8	3 11
A 60	22	3	5 6	3 1
B 60	34	5	5 6	3 1
C 60	110	5	5 6	3 1
		19	5 6	3 1

---

[12] A small closet containing two beds, opening of No. 13, is not included. 13 and 14 are prisoners' wards.

The data in this table are sufficient to show the extraordinary irregularity of the building. The wards are of all sizes and heights, and afford every variety of cubic space and superficial area to the sick. In most of the wards both of these requisites are very much greater than would be necessary in a properly constructed hospital.

But on the other hand most of the cubic space is useless for any sanitary purpose, as it is quite above the beds, and from 15 to 30 feet above the point where it would be useful to the patients. The great breadth of the lower wards, and the consequent distance between opposite windows, are also most injurious to ventilation.

Another remarkable point is the entire disproportion between the window-space and the cubic contents of the wards. About 50 square feet of window-space for every 3,000 cubic feet of contents are necessary to admit the required amount of light and air to sick wards in such a climate as Malta; while the window-space of the more important wards is only from one-fifteenth to one-twentieth part of this proportionate area, and as a consequence the wards are dark and dismal, besides being close, and the air always more or less stagnant. The windows, small as they are, are all close to the roof, so that there is nothing for the sick to look at, not even the sky, besides the dead walls and their sick comrades opposite. Medical officers complain of the bad moral effect produced on the sick by the want of light and view, and state that their patients come gradually to concentrate their whole thoughts on their maladies.

In so far as regards the sanitary state of the hospital, arising out of its site and construction, there cannot be a doubt that it is very bad. Sick men recover very slowly in it. Zymotic diseases, such as fevers, become more severe and fatal while the sick are in it, and pass from the simple continued into the typhoid form. All this has been long known to observing medical officers; and lately it has been found necessary to open a sanitarium, as it is called, at Citta Vecchia, while they linger or die in the general hospital. This is a sure mark of the real state of the place, and of its unfitness for sick.

AN
ACCOUNT
OF THE PRINCIPAL
LAZARETTOS
IN
EUROPE;
WITH VARIOUS PAPERS RELATIVE TO THE
PLAGUE:
TOGETHER WITH FURTHER OBSERVATIONS ON SOME
FOREIGN PRISONS AND HOSPITALS;
AND ADDITIONAL REMARKS
ON THE PRESENT STATE OF THOSE IN
GREAT BRITAIN AND IRELAND.

BY JOHN HOWARD, F.R.S.

THE SECOND EDITION, WITH ADDITIONS.

"O let the sorrowful sighing of the PRISONERS come before thee."

LONDON:
PRINTED FOR J. JOHNSON, C. DILLY, AND T. CADELL.
M.DCC.XCI.

But more than this, during the last epidemic of cholera at Malta, most of the cases among the troops happened in the general hospital; just where they might have been expected to happen.

NOTE D

HOWARD'S LAZARETTOS IN EUROPE, 1789 (p. 58). MALTA.

"The hospital *(de St Jean de Jerusalem)* for men is situated near the water. The three principal wards are in the form of a T, which communicate one with another, having an altar in the centre. By additional buildings the ward on one side is made longer than that on the other. Their breadth is 34,5 feet, but the cross ward is only 29 feet 4 inches wide. These three wards, connected, are called the hall. The pavement is of neat marble (or stone) squares. The ceiling is lofty, but, being wood, now turned black; the windows being small, and the walls hung round with dusty pictures, this noble hall makes but a gloomy appearance. All the patients lie single. One ward is for patients dangerously sick or dying, another for patients of the middle rank of life, and the third for the lower and poorer sort of patients. In this last ward (which is the largest) there were four rows of beds, in the others only two. They were all so dirty and offensive as to create the necessity of perfuming them; and yet I observed that the physician, in going his rounds, was obliged to keep his handkerchief to his face. The use of perfume I always reckon a proof of inattention to cleanliness and airiness; and this inattention struck me forcibly on opening some of the private closets, with which this hall is very properly furnished. There are several other wards, and some single rooms for such of the knights as choose to come here when sick. There is likewise a large apartment in which the governor (always one of the knights) resides during the time of his being governor, which is two years. He has a salary; and is generally, as a sensible gentleman here told me, a young and inexperienced person, others either not liking the confinement, or being fearful of catching some distemper.

"The great hall already mentioned is on the ground-floor, and under it is another hall, or rather a large ward, which is nothing but a dark and damp arched cellar. Here were cutaneous patients, also fifty-two infirm servants from the city, who are maintained by the Religion. The first and the under physician, with the surgeon, a few pupils, and one or two attendants, take the round or walk of the upper wards, but in this ward the first physician does not attend. In the great hall there is a slate fixed on the closet door at the side of the beds of the patients, on which the initial letters of their usual medicines, diet, &c., are written. On this slate, also, one of the pupils always marks the doctor's order, so that at his next visit, he may see his last prescription. When these gentlemen go their rounds, the patients are all required to be in their beds.

"The patients are twice a-day, at eight and four, served with provisions: one of the knights and the under physician constantly attending in the two halls, and seeing the distribution. From the kitchen (which is darker and more offensive than even the lower hall, to which it adjoins), the broth, rice, soup, and vermicelli are brought in dirty kettles first to the upper hall, and there poured into three silver bowls, out of which the patients are served. They who are in the ward for the very sick, and those of the middle rank of life, are served in plates, dishes, and spoons of silver; but the other patients (who are far the most numerous) are served on pewter. I objected to the sweet-cakes and two sorts of clammy sweetmeats which were given to the patients.

"The number of patients in this hospital during the time I was at Malta (29th March to 19th April 1786) was from 510 to 532. These were served by the most dirty, ragged, unfeeling, and inhuman persons I ever saw. I once found 8 or 9 of them highly entertained with a delirious dying patient. The governor told me they had only 22 servants, and that many of them were debtors or criminals, who had fled thither for refuge. At the same time I observed that near 40 attendants were kept to take charge of about 26 horses and the same number of mules in the Grand Master's stables, and that there all was clean. I cannot help adding that in the centre of each of these stables there was a fountain, out of which water was constantly running into a stone basin; but that in the hospital, though there was indeed a place for a fountain, there was no water.

"There is a great want of room in this hospital. I requested that a delirious patient who disturbed the other patients, might be lodged in a room by himself, but was told that no such room could be found. Opposite to this hospital there is a large house, which is now used only for a wash-house. A great improvement might be made by providing a wash-house for the hospital somewhere out of the city (its only proper situation), and appropriating these spacious and airy apartments to poor knights and convalescent patients. The slow hospital fever (the inevitable consequence of closeness, uncleanliness, and dirt) prevails here.

"At the back of the hall, over the knights' arms (a cross), is a marble crown, and under it on white marble, is this inscription -

"INTFANTIUM INCOLUMITATI"

Here is a wooden cradle, which, turning on an axis, the pins strike a bell, to give notice of the reception of infants into the Foundling Hospital. These infants, after being received, are sent to the governess of that hospital, who provides nurses for them in the country; and on the first Sunday in every month these nurses bring back the children to show them, and at the same time to receive their pay; the governess, very properly, being present. On one of these occasions I had the pleasure of seeing a number of fine healthy children.

"In the hospital for women there were 230 patients, who had all separate beds. The governess attended me through every ward, and was constantly using her smelling-bottle; in which she judged very properly, for a more offensive and dirty hospital for women I never visited.

"Sir William Hamilton favoured me with a letter to the Grand Master, which I presented after my first visit to this great hospital. He very kindly and readily said that the prisons and hospitals should be all open to me. On a subsequent visit, he asked me what I thought of his Hospitals? I faithfully told his Highness my sentiments, and made some of the remarks that I now publish; adding, that if he himself would sometimes walk over the hospitals, many abuses would be corrected. But my animadversions were reckoned too free: yet, being encouraged by the satisfaction which the patients seemed to receive from my frequent visits, I continued them; and I have reason to believe they produced an alteration for the better in the state of these hospitals, with respect to cleanliness and attention to the patients.

"In the Foundling Hospital there were 39 girls, from seven to about twelve years of age, who were clean both in their persons and dress, but very pale. They have no proper place for exercise, and but two bedrooms, one of which is close and offensive. A piece of ground, which might contribute to their health by being made a play-ground, is a sort of useless garden.

"Near the city there are two Houses for the Poor. In that for men there were 140 poor persons, who are lodged in eight or nine rooms in a range, on the ground-floor; with a church appropriated to them, and apartments for a chaplain adjoining. Their allowance is a brown loaf (weight exactly 1,5 lb.), some soup, and a little cheese, and on some days a penny in money; and many of them have a small garden. There being no common hall or dining-room, every one carries his provision into his bedroom. On the whole, however, these infirm persons are pretty well supplied and accommodated.

"In the house for women there were 213, to whom a kind attention seems to be paid by the governor, who has convenient apartments adjoining.

"Before I leave Malta I would just mention that the staircase at the Grand Master's palace is the most convenient for infirm persons that I have ever seen; from which hints may be taken for the more easy ascent to the upper wards in our hospitals. It is circular, 9 feet 3 inches wide, the rises 2,5 inches, the steps at the widest end 2 feet 2 inches, and at the narrowest 9 inches."

NOTE E

EXTRACTS FROM THE REPORT OF Mr THORNTON, AUDITOR-GENERAL, UPON THE FINANCES OF MALTA

"The estates of the Order in 1788 spread through Europe, administered through 29 agencies *(ricetti)*, from Lisbon to Warsaw, by receivers, who had to collect responsions *(responsioni)*, entrances *(passagi)*, effects of the dead *(spogli)*, and all commanderies vacant *(mortori e vacanti)*. Besides these, there were others 'in convent' *i.e.*, at headquarters, chiefly the letting of property there.
"The annual revenue amounted to 1,315,299 scudi. The expenditure on the great hospital was 79,476 scudi; on the hospital for women, 18,677 scudi (1500 scudi being added from another fund): and for foundlings and children of indigent parents, 6147 scudi; each individual costing the treasury from 5 to 6 tari a-day. The repairs at the hospital in 1776 amounted to 7225 scudi. A small house bought for the hospital in 1781 cost 1854 scudi. The plate at the hospital was valued in 1788 at 34,498 scudi. In 1796 the hospital foundlings and alms stand at 146,481 scudi.

"Antonine *Order.* - In 1095 the nobles of Dauphigny founded a fraternity of Hospitallers, erected into a regular Order in 1218 for the relief of sufferers under St Anthony's Fire. In 1777 this Order was united with that of St John, and its property taken possession of, subject to various life-pensions, changes, and conditions. The compliance with these terms, as well as the conventions made with parties interested in the Antonine estates, with a view to free possession at a future day, involved an excess of expenditure which during ten years amounted to 732,947 scudi; and it was calculated that an excess of expenditure would continue, with gradual diminution until 1794, when a net income would return, and go on increasing till 1879, when the outlay, with interest, would be recovered to the treasury, and the annual income reach 120,000 French livres. The Antonine estates were situated in France and Savoy. In 1792 the property of the Order in France was confiscated. Thus, not only the members of the Order belonging to the three Langues of France, Auvergne, and Provence, lost the income from their commanderies, but the Order lost its revenues from responsions and other dues of the estates, a sum estimated at 471,784 scudi, exclusive of the Antonine estates, upon which the Order, up to 1792, must have lost a million scudi."

Note F

COATS OF ARMS AND INSCRIPTIONS IN UPPER WARD OF HOSPITAL

All the escutcheons are upon the cross of the Order, and with a chief gules, a cross argent, as Priors.

I. (On right of arch) 1. arg., a lion rampant gu., crowned or, quartering; 2. az., three fleurs-de-lys or; 3. or, a fess checky arg. and gu.; 4. az. semée-de-lys, two dolphins endorsed or; 5. gu., a cross arg. ; 6. az., a lion rampant arg.; 7. Barry of eight, arg. and gu., a lion rampant, sable; 8. az., six plates in pile, and a chief or; on an escutcheon of pretence or, two cows passant gu.; supporters, two griffins.
 F. HENRI AUGUSTE BEON DE LUXEMBOURG. - A gouvernè l'Infirmerie depuis le 11 Juillet 1681, jusqu'au 18 Mai 1683.

II. (On left of doorway) az. (defaced); supporters, two eagles proper. No inscription.

III. Az., three bezants between nine crescents arg.
F. HEROSME FRANCOIS DE LA CHAUSSEE D'ARREST. - A gouvernè l'Infirmerie depuis le 18 Mai 1701, jusqu'au 18 Mai 1707.

IV. Gu., three mallets or.
F. GEO. FRANCOIS DE MOUELNY DE VIMES. - A gouvernè l'Infirmerie depuis le 18 Mai 1705, jusqu'au 18 Mai 1707.

V. Barry of eight, arg. and sable, ten martlets in pile of the second.F. FRANCOIS DE NOSSAY. - À gouvernè l'Infirmerie depuis le 18 Mai 1707, jusqu'au 5 Octobre 1710. Jour de sa mort.

VI. Arg., a chevron sable, between three trefoils vert.
F. GUILLAUME FRANÇOIS DE BERNART DAVEMES DE BOCAGE, COMMANDEUR D'ORLEANS. - A gouvernè l'Infirmerie depuis le 6 Octobre 1710, jusqu'au 6 Avril 1716.

VII. Or, fretty gu., in each fret a hurt; on a base of the first, a label reversed of the second; supporters, two griffins or.
F. MICHEL PHILIPPE DE MAILLE DE JOUR LANDRY. - A gouvernè l'Infirmerie depuis le 6 Avril 1716, jusqu'au 6 Avril 1720.

VIII. Az., a lion rampant or.

F. VICTOR HENRY LE ROUX DE LA CORLIMIERE. - A gouvernè l'Infirmerie depuis le 6 Avril 1720, jusqu'au 14 Avril 1722.

IX. Arg., a lion rampant az.; supporters, two lions or.
F. VICTOR FERA DE ROUVILLE. - A gouvernè l'Infirmerie depuis le 14 Avril 1722, jusqu'au 6 Avril 1724.

X. Arg., on a fess gu., three crosslets or, in chief three martlets sable; supporters, two savage men wreathed vert, each with club on his shoulder, proper.
LE CHEVALIER F. EMMANUEL PHILIPPE DE BRUNE. - A gouvernè l'Infirmerie depuis le 6 Avril 1724, jusqu'au 6 Avril 1726.

XI. Gu., three six-foils az.; supporters, two lions or.
LE CHEVALIER F. JACQUES FRANCOIS QUINNEBAUD DE LA GROSTIERE. - A gouvernè l'Infirmerie depuis le 6 Avril 1726, jusqu'au 6 Avril 1730.

XII. Or, two lozenges az., on a chief of the second, two bezants.
F. AIME CHARLES DE LUDERT. - A gouvernè l'Infirmerie depuis le 17 Avril 1730, jusqu'au 6 Avril 1732.

XIII. Az., a lion salient or.
F. FRANÇOIS NICOLAS DE LA DIVE. - A gouvernè l'Infirmerie depuis le 6 Avril 1732, jusqu'au 6 Avril 1734. Etant nommé par Monsieur le Chevalier de la Roche Brochard, Commandeur de Villegats.

XIV. Arg., a lion rampant sable; supporters, two griffins or.
F. PIERRE DE POLLASTRON. - À gouvernè l'Infirmerie depuis le 6 Avril 1734, jusqu'au 0 Avril 1730.

XV. Party per pale, arg. and gu., three crosslets in chief, az.
F. ALEXIS BINET BE MONTIFROY. - A gouvernè l'Infirmerie depuis le 17 Mars 1741, jusqu'au 17 Mars 1743.

XVI. Az., three eaglets displayed in fess, arg.
F. ALEXANDRE DE LA HAYE. - A gouvernè l'Infirmerie, depuis le 17 Mars 1743, jusqu'au 17 Mars 1747.

XVII. Az., two swords in saltire, points downwards, proper, hilts or.
F. RENE BERNARD DE MARBEUF. - A gouvernè l'Infirmerie depuis le 17 Mars 1747, jusqu'au 17 Mars 1749.

XVIII.Arg., three bends az.; on a chief gu., a lion passant-guardant, crowned or.
F. GEORGE HENRI LOUIS DES VERRIERES. - A gouvernè l'Infirmerie depuis le 3 Octobre 1755, jusqu'au 3 Octobre 1765.
At end of ward.

ET NOS DEBEMUS ANIMAS PRO FRATIBUS PONERE. – JOAN. c. iii.

COAT OF ARMS IN GREAT CORRIDOR OF HOSPITAL.

Gu., a cross arg., for the Order+; quartering, arg., three fleurs-de-lys or. Supporters, two hands and arms issuing from clouds, holding swords erect, proper.
These have been conjectured to be intended for the arms of France, in allusion to the privilege which the French Langue possessed of appointing the Hospitaller; but if such had been the intention, they would hardly have been quartered with the arms of the Order, in the manner restricted to Grand Masters. It is more probable that they were intended for the arms of G.M. Vignacourt (az., 3 fleurs-de-lys couped at foot, or), and erroneously blazoned. The error of argent for azure is transparent.

NOTE G

STATEMENT OF PROPERTY TRANSFERRED TO MILITARY AND NAVAL AUTHORITIES (MALTA 1877).

"General Hospital, Strada Mercanti, 115.
"Fondato nel 1578. Fabbricato sopra il sito acio reservato in parte dal Gran Maestro Levesque de la Cassiere (ingrandito sotto il Gran Maestro Raffalle Cotoner a speso del Tesoro) ed in parie dalla Religione ad uso degli animalati fratelli e secolari.
"Riedificato nel 1662 ed una casa vicina dalla parte del rastrello fu incorporata all detto Ospedale nel 1780 a spese del Tesoro. Il detto Ospedale eza amministrato da una congregazione composta dal Yen: Ospedeliare, due Gran Croci, e quattro Cavalieri, ed eza matenuto dalla Religione."

NOTE H:

In 1796, Regulations "for the Spiritual, Political, and Economical Government of the Hospital" were promulgated, involving some changes in its administration, and in the details of the service, &c.
Thirty-eight attendants are thus distributed, Sala Grande, *four;* S. Vecchia, *two;* S. Nuova, *two*; S. Feriti, *two;* Saletta or Sala S. Giuseppe, *three;* Magazine, *seven;* Lucina, *six;* Bottighliera, *two;* Lingeria, *ten.* These were to he paid weekly at the rate of 3 tari and 18 grani a-day. It was proposed to give the dispenser 57 scudi a-month, and the assistance of six laveranti, and two gazzonè, at salaries varying from 16 scudi 6 tari, to 8 scudi a-month. The number of patients is stated to be ordinarily from 350 to 400. The summary of the annual accounts, from May 1, 1795, to April 30, 1796, gives an expenditure for food - viz., baked bread, wine, oil, flour, raisins, meat, and vermicelli - of 48,866 scudi.

NOTE I

EXTRACT FROM ST PRIEST'S TRAVELS IN MALTA, 1791.

"L'hospital conteint plusieurs grands salles bien aerees et de vastes magazine dans lequels on peut a l'aise quadrupler les rangs de lits: dans cet asile ouvert aux malhereux de tous les pays, de toutes les religions, de tous les cultes on prodigue aux malades les soins les remedes les consolations des chevaliers, y surveillent non seulement les diverses parties d'administration, dont la premiere place est une de grandes dignitès de l'Ordre, mais tous y vont eux memes servir les malades. La vaisselle qu' on y employe est presque toute en argent, la simplicite de son travail annonce que cette magnificence est moins un objet de luxe qu' un moyen de proprete. "

Order of St John of Jerusalem in England. 1881.

This Order was founded about the year 1092, for the maintenance of an hospital at Jerusalem; and, subsequently, the defence of Christian pilgrims on their journeys to and from the Holy Land. It afterwards became a knightly institution; but ever preserved its hospitals, and cherished the duty of alleviating sickness and suffering.

The Order was first planted in England in the year 1100, and raised the noble structure which once formed the Priory of Clerkenwell, of which the gateway now alone remains to attest the importance of the chief house of the Order in England.

The Order held high place in this country until the year 1540, when it was despoiled, suppressed, and its property confiscated by Act of Parliament. In 1557 it was restored by Royal Charter, and much of its possessions regranted; but only to be again confiscated within the subsequent two years by a second statute, which did not, however, enact the resuppression of the fraternity. Still, with the loss of possessions, and the withdrawal of most of its members to Malta - then the sovereign seat of the Order - it became practically dormant in England.

Many fluctuations have marked the fortunes of an institution which played a prominent part in most of the great events of Europe, until its supreme disaster in the loss of Malta, in 1798; after, which the surviving divisions of the Order had each to perpetuate an independent existence, and to mark out the course of its own future.

It is now nearly half a century ago that a majority of five of the seven then existing remnants of the institution decreed the revival of the time-honoured branch of the Order in England; since which event it has, so far as means permitted, pursued, in spirit, the original purposes of its foundation - the alleviation of the sick and suffering of the human race.

The following are some of the objects which have engaged the attention of the Order: -
Providing convalescent patients of hospitals (without distinction of creed) with such nourishing diets as are medically ordered; so as to aid their return, at the earliest possible time, to the business of life and the support of their families.
The (original) institution in England of what is now known as the "National Society for Aid to Sick and Wounded in War."
The foundation and maintenance of Cottage Hospitals and Convalescent' Homes.
Providing the means and opportunities for local training of nurses for the sick poor; and the foundation of what is now known as the Metropolitan and National Society for training and supplying such nurses.
The promotion of a more intimate acquaintance with the wants of the poor in time of sickness.
The establishment of ambulance-litters, for the conveyance of sick and injured persons, in the colliery and mining districts, and in all large railway and other public departments and towns, as a means of preventing much aggravation of human suffering.
The award of silver and bronze medals, and certificates of honour, for special services on land in the cause of humanity.
The initiation and organisation, during the recent Turco-Servian War, of the "Eastern Wax Sick and Wounded Relief Fund. "
The institution of the "St John Ambulance Association" for instruction in the preliminary treatment of the Injured in Peace and the Wounded in War.
Although started more than three years since, this latter movement has already attained very great success, and upwards of 100 Local Centres have already been formed in important towns and districts in all parts of the kingdom, many others being in course of formation. Among the more notable classes are those for the instruction of the Metropolitan and City Police; County Constabulary; London and Provincial Fire Brigades; Royal Naval Artillery Volun-

teers; the War Office; Admiralty; Somerset House ; and other Government Departments ; the Custom House; East and West India Docks; Surrey Commercial Docks; Victoria Docks; and numerous public and private institutions. It is only necessary to add, as a further proof of the value of the movement, that several members of the Royal Family - H.R.H. the Duke of Edinburgh, H.R.H Prince Leopold, and H.R.H. Prince, and Princess Christian - hold the offices of Presidents, or Patrons, of Country Centres.

Detached classes have also been held, pending the formation of Centres, at many other places.

Amongst many important public meetings held in connection with this branch of the Order two deserve special mention, not only on account of the additional impetus thereby given to the work, but also as indicating, in an unmistakable manner, the growing interest taken by all classes in its development.

On the 15th February last, a most enthusiastic meeting, numerously attended, was held at the Mansion House, by the kind permission, and under the presidency of, the Lord Mayor, chiefly with a view of extending the work more fully in the City and Port of London.

On the 19th April H.R.H. the Princess Mary of Cambridge, Duchess of Teck, presented Certificates to successful pupils [principally ladies and policemen] at the Town Hall, Kensington, in the presence of a large and distinguished audience.

The Order of St John has no connection whatever with any of the numerous associations or fraternities now existing for benevolent or other purposes, whether similar or not in name; nor is it allied with any sect or party of any one religious denomination, but is thoroughly universal - embracing among its members and associates those who, in the spirit of our Divine Master, are willing to devote a portion of their time or their means to the help of the suffering and the sick.

St John's Gate, Clerkenwell,
August 1881.

Lord Prior.

His Grace William Drogo, Duke of Manchester, K.P.

Bailiff of Eagle.

The Right Hon. William Henry, Baron Leigh.

Commander of Hanley Castle.

Sir Edmund A.H. Lechmere, Bart, M.P., F.S.A.

The Council.

President - General Sir John St George, K.C.B.
    Major-General the Most Honble. the Marquis of Conyngham.
    The Right Honourable the Earl of Dudley.
    The Right Rev. the Lord Bishop of St Albans.
        (*Chaplain- General*).
    Sir Edward G.L. Perrot, Bart.
    Colonel Sir James Bourne, Bart., C.B., F.S.A.
    General Sir H. C. B. Daubeney, K.C.B.
    John Furley, Esq.

Executive Officers.
Who are *ex officio* Members of the Council.

Chancellor - General Sir John St George, KC.B.
Secretary and Receiver - Sir E. A. H. Lechmere, Bart., M.P., F.S.A.
Registrar - Lieut.-Colonel Gould Hunter-Weston, F.S.A.
Almoner - General the Viscount Templetown, K.C.B.
Sub-Almoner - Capt. James Gildea, 4th Batt. Royal Warwickshire Regt.

Genealogist - Rev. W. K. R. Bedford, M.A.
Librarian – Edwin Freshfield, Esq. M.A., V.P.S.A.
Assistant Secretary – CaptainPerrott, 3d Batt. East Kent Regt.
Ambulance Department - Director: Major F. DUNCAN, R.A., M.A, D.C.L.

Bankers - The London and Westminster Bank, 1 St James's Square, S.W.

Communications may be addressed to the Secretary of the Order of St John, St John's Gate, Clerkenwell, London, E.C.

139

TAVOLA PER L'INFERMERIA.

Officiali, p.3[1]	Ecclesiastici.	Medici.	Chirurghi.	Speziaria.	Numero delle Sale.		Letti.
Il Gran Ospidaliere.	Priore, che hà il servente Frà Cap. Convent.	Medici primarü trè.	Chirurghi principali che tagliano pietra etc. trè.	Officiali speziale, e cinque ajutanti.	Sala per li cavalierie e due camere per feriti.		Per li cavalieri.
Infermiere Cavaliere per il buon governo.	Sotto – Priore Frà Cap. d'-Ubb.	Medici prattici due.	Prattici di chirurgia due.	Si danno gratis medicamenti à altri mali.	Sale grande per febri, e		Seccolari, e persone civili.
Due Prodomi per l'economia	Otto Sacerdoti Frà Cap. d'-Ubb.	Lettore pubblico di anotomia.	Barberotti ajutanti sei.	Quattro monasteri di monache.	Sala vecchia per le persone civili.		Con padiglione, 369.
Amoriere Frà servante, per custodier l'argenteria	Sagrestano.	Accademia pubblica per ogni Setimana. Pag. 6.	Barbiere fisico. Due ajutanti per fisca.	Quattro conservatorij due di S. Enizia che si mantiene avendone fondato uno, e uno	Saletta per li moribondi, e due camere.		Senza padiglione, 365. Pag.8.
Scrivano dell'Abito, per i conti Fràservente.	Il papas Greco viene per li Greci dalla sua Parrochia.		Una donna per curare i poveri della Tigna, ed altro.	chè si dice del Chiesa. Casa di Ripentite.	Sala nuova e due camere per il taglio della pietra.		

[1] The numbers (pag. 3, &c.) refer to the pages in the original text

Officiali, p.3[1]	Ecclesiasti-ci.	Medici.	Chirurghi.	Speziaria.	Numero delle Sale.	Letti.
Srivano dé Prodomi. Lingiere per custodir la biancheria, ed altro.	Pag. 5.		Pag. 7.	P.P. Capuccini. P. P. Teresiani.	Sala dei feriti condue camere. Salone per le genti di catina. Camere due. Sale due per li spalmanti nelle Falanca.	
Bottigliere per dispensare, pane, vino, ed altro.				P.P. Zoccolanti Tutti i poveri e povere. Pag.7.	Camere per la stufa fuori dell' Infermeria	
Scrivanello per la lista della mangia. Due cuochi per la cucina. Compratore per la rabba, e compagni. Guardiani 14; stuffarolo, 1. Portieri, 3. Schiavi battezzati, 14; schiavi Turchi e forzati, 30.					Pag.8.	

141

Lenzuola.	Coperte.	Argenteria.	Arazzi.	Quadri.	Qualità di Pitanze.	Rinfreschi.
Per cavalieri e religiosi,	Per Cavalieri e religiosi.	Scodelle, 250. Pag. 9.	Tapezzaria per l'Inverno.	Per gl'altari.	Consumato di gallina, erbette, vermicelli.	Restauranti
Per secolari, regolari, e gente di catena.	Per regolari, e secolari, gente di catena.	Piatti, 356.	Pezze, 131.	Per le sale.	Riso, pisti, piccatigli, frigassia, ed altro.	Biscottini.
In tutto, 1517.	In tutto, 1141.	Piatti grandi, 1.	Pag. 10.	In tutto, 85.	Gallina, piccioni, pollastri, caccia, vitella, vitellazza.	Pomicotti e granati con zucchero e altre confeture.
		Tazze, 167. Bacili grandi, 3. Bacilotti, 12. Cocchiaroni, 10. Forchette, 10.			Amandolata, ova fresche, prugna, zibibo, alli cavalieri si dà pitanza doppia. Pag.11.	

Lenzuola.	Coperte.	Argenteria.	Arazzi.	Quadri.	Qualità di Pitanze.	Rinfreschi
		Quartucci, 43, Tazze a becco, 4. Vasi a becco, 1. Scatola, 1 Lampade, 13. Pignatte grandi, e piccole, 8. Bocali, 4. Sottocoppa 1. Oltre l'argenteria della Capella. Si suplisce anche con stagno.				

Camicie.	Assistenza de Fratelli.	Sepoltura.	Elemosine fisse.		Elemosine estraorde.	Spesa Annua comprese tutte le spese.
Alli poveri che vengono logori, e stracciati si dispensa una camiscia che conduca seco.	I Fratelli dell'Ordine Gerosolimitano portano il mangiare a malati.	Li cavalieri defonti si portano da sei cavalieri a San Giovanni.	A ciechi, stroppi, leprosi, ed altro, e altri invalidi ogni mese importano, scudi 100.		Consumato, e vermicelli che si dispensano a povere.	Importa in circa, scudi di rame sessanta mila, 60,000 scudi. Pag. 12.
Camicie, 160 ogni anno. Pag. 10.	La Domenica servono li cavalieri di Provenza. Lunedi quelli d'Alvernia. Martedi quelli di Francia. Mercoldi gl'Italiani. Giovedi, Aragona. Venerdi Alemagna.	Li servitori e famigliari de'cavalieri alla Vittoria. Il rimanente nel cimitero dell'Infermeria. Pag. 11.	Alla Bormola, scudi 57, alla settimana Santa. A sette zitelle esposte la dote di scudi 50 ogni una. Pag. 12.		Brachieri, stampelle bastoni, ed altro. Altri per morte, o mancanza di latte de' primi Parenti. Mangiare a Capuccini infermi. P.P. Teresiani. Maroniti. Missionarij, ed altro.	

Camicie	Assistenza de Fratelli.	Sepoltura.	Elemosine fisse.	Elemosine estraorde.	Spesa Annua comprese tutte le spese.
	Sabato quelli di Castiglia e Portugallo. Li Novizzi distribuiti nell'istessa maniera. Pag.10			Imbarco che si dà ai missionarj. Stanza letto, e pitanza à pellegrani, ed alt. Pag.12.	

TAVOLA PER LA CARICA DELLI COMMISSARJ DELLE POVERE INFERME.

Regolamento per le Povere Inferme.	Medici.	Chirurgi.	Medicamenti.	Pitanze.	Pane fisso.
Officiali. Pag. 13	Per la città Va-lletta due.	Per la città Va-lletta due.	Per tutte le povere delle qua-ttro città.	Alle più grave un tari e un pari di pane.	Per le povere delle quattro città.
Due cavalieri di differente nazione commissarj delle povere inferme dell'Isola.	Uno per il Borgo.	Uno per il Borgo.	Dell'Isola di Malte e Gozzo.	Alle meno un carline, e il pane il giorno.	Pane fisso paracento cinguanta il giorno: para 150.
Scrivano per li conti dei sudetti commissarj. Pag. 14.	Uno per l'Isola.	Uno per l'Isola.	Oltre li soliti si danno anche Decotti, brodi, ed altro.	Dissutili tutte due la sittimana, e il pane giornale.	Pag. 15.
Quattro pitanzerie per distribuire le pitanze per le quattro città. Pag. 14.	Uno per Bormola. Pag. 14	Uno per Bormola. Pag. 14	Toltone a donne pubbliche, che devono andare all'Incurabile volendosi curare. Pag. 14	Vecchie un paro di pane il giorno.	
E quattro donne ajutanti.				I tutto ascendono al numero di 150 il giorno. Pag. 15.	

Mesate fisse.	Casetta ò Incurabile.	Ecclesiastico.	Medici e Chirurgi.	Medicamenti.	Qualità di Pitanze.
A povere disutili che sono diverse per tutte le città.	La Sacra Religione mantiene la detta Casa.	Un prete soggetto all'Ordinario lasciato dalla Religione.	Li due medici delle povere della città.	Medicamenti della speziara dell'Infermeria, e tutte le sorte con firma del commissario.	Ottimo consumato minestre di zuppa.
In tutte le città sono scudi 60, in 70 il mese.	Officiali. Li due commissarj delle povere.	Pag. 17.	Li due chirurgi per le povere della medesima.		Gnocchetti tagliolini tutte forti di pasta riso.
Pag. 15.	Uno scrivano per li conti. Uno per la mancia.		Pag. 17.	Pag. 17.	Gallina. Piccione. Pollastro. Vitella. Vitellazza. Polpetie.
	Barberotto ò spezia-lotto per li medica-menti. Una governatri-ce. Quattro serve. Una croce. Un famiglio.				Frigassia. Stuffato. Ova. Amendolata. Prugna. Passoli. Restauranti. Biscottini. Vino buono. e altri rifreschi.
	Pag. 16.				Pag. 18.

Numero delle Sale.	Unzione mercuriale.	Elemosine fisse.	Spesa Annua.	Li Medici e Chirurghi sono pagati dal comune Tesoro.
Sala per li decotti.	Due volte l'anno Maggio, e Settembre.	L'esposte della Falanca si curano nell'Incurabile.	Senza li medicamenti.	Li medicamenti si uniscono con il conto dell'Infermeria.
Sala vecchia per le febbricitanti.	Non si rifi-uta nessu-na. Pag. 19.	Siriceovno le vecchie e dissutili	Senza il pane ne fisso ne, ed altro.	
Sala delle spalmanti.		Pazze e povere parturienti vergognose.	Senza li salarj de' medici e chirurghi.	
Sala delle ferite. Sala delle vecchie. Pag. 18.		Si dispensa la minestra, e pane che resta ad altre povere che ivi vengono. Pag. 19.	In tutto spendono li commissarj in circa scudi tremila nove cento l'anno. Pag. 19.	_____Sc. 3900.

TABLE FOR THE INFIRMARY.

Officers.	Ecclesiastics.	Doctors	Surgeons.	Apothecary.	No. of Wards.	Beds.
The Great Hospitaller.	The Prior, having an assistant Conventual *frère* Chaplain.	Three principal doctors.	Three principal surgeons for lithotomy.	Official chemist and five assistants.	The knights ward, and two rooms for the wounded.	For the knights.
Infermiere – a knight, to keep order.	Sub-Prior, *frère* chaplain of Obedience.	Two practical doctors.	Two practical surgeons..	Medicines are distributed gratis to the	Large ward for fever and other maladies.	Laity and private persons.
Two *Prodomi* for management.	Eight priests, *frère* chaplains of Obedience. Sacristan.	Practical lecturer of anatomy.	Two assistants in phlebotomy.	Four monasteries for nuns.	Old ward for private persons	With curtains, 369.
Amoriere fra-servente to be in charge of plate.	The Greek priest comes from his own parish to attend those of that Church.	Public academy every week. Page 6.	Medical phlebotomist. Two assistant physicians. One woman to attend the poor at the Falanga.	Four poorhouses, one of which was founded by his Eminence and another is called after the Prior of the Church. The house of Penitents	Small ward and two rooms for dying people. New ward and two rooms for lithotomy. Ward for the wounded and two rooms.	Without curtains, 365. Page 8.
Clerk of the Habit for the accouts, *fra-servente*.						

149

Officers.	Eccles-tiastics.	Doc-tors	Sur-geons.	Apothecary.	No. of Wards.	Beds
Clerk of the *Prodomi*. *Lingiere* to take care of linen, &c. Lingiere to take care of linen, &c.	Page 5.		Page 7.	Capuchin Friars, Teresian Fathers.	Large ward for the slaves. Two Wards and rooms for the anoint-ers in the Falanga.	
Bottigliere to give away bread, wine &c.				Franziscan Friars. Male and female poor.	Hot bath-room outside the Infer-mary.	
Petty clerk to make the list of the *mancia*. Two cooks for the kitchen. Purveyor and assistants to buy goods, &c. Warders 14; bathman 1. Doorkeepers 3. Portieri, 3. Baptised slaves 14;Turkish slaves – con-victs,30.				Page 7.	Page 8.	

Sheets.	Coverlets.	Plate.	Tapestry.	Pictures.	Quality of Allowances.	Refreshments.
For the knights and religious people.	For the knights and religious people.	Bowls, 250. Page 9.	Winter Tapestry.	For the altars.	Soups made of gallinas, herbs and vermicelli.	Restoratives and refreshments.
For laity and monastic people, and slaves.	laity, monastic people and slaves.	Dishes, 356.	131 Pieces.	For the wards.	Rice, minced meat, fricassees	Biscuits.
Altogether, 1517.	Altogether, 1141.	Large dishes, 1.	Page 10.	Total, 85.	Fowls, pigeons, gallinas, game, veals, beef.	Baked apples, pomegranates with sugar.
		Cups, 167. Large basins, 3. Small basins, 12. Spoons, 256. Large spoons, 10. Forks, 10.			Almonds, pastry, fresh eggs, plums, raisins. Double quantity is given to the knights. Page 11.	And other sorts of confections.

151

Sheets.	Coverlets.	Plate.	Tapestry.	Pictures.	Quality of Allowances.	Refreshments.
		Quart-measures, 43. Drinking-cups, 14. Drinking-vessels, 1. Casket, 1 Lamps, 13. Pots, in sizes small and large, 18. Jugs, 4. Salver, 1. Besides the plate for the use of the Chapel. Pewter is supplied for other purposes.				

Shirts.	Assistance of the Brothers.	Burial.	Ordinary Alms.	Extraordinary Alms.	Annual Expense, all the expense included.
To worn and raged poor, one shirt is given to be taken away with them.	The Brothers of the Order of Jerusalem carry the food to the sick.	The dead knights are carried to St. John's Church by six knights.	The amount of money spent monthly in alms to the blind, lame, leprous, is 100 *scudi*.	Strong broth and vermicelli are distributed to the poor old women..	The expense comes to nearly 60,000 *scudi* in copper. Page 12.
Every year 160 shirts are distributed. Page 10.	On Sunday the knights of Provence are duty. On Monday the knights of Auvergne. On Tuesday those of France. On Wednesday those of Italy. On Thursday those of Aragon. On Friday those of Germani.	Servants and domestics of the knights to Vittoriosa. Others in the cemetery of the Infirmary. Page 11.	To Burmola, 100 *scudi* in holy Week. To seven foundling spinsters a dowry of 50 *scudi* each. Page 12.	Trusses, crutches, sticks, &c. Aid to others (infants) whose parents are dead or cannot give them milk. Food is given to the sick Capuchins. To the Teresian Fathers. Maronites, missionaries, &c. expenses of embarkation. Rooms, beds, and allowances to the pilgrims &c.	

Shirts.	Assistance of the Brothers.	Burial.	Ordinary Alms.	Extraordinary Alms.	Annual Expense, all the expense included.
	On Saturday those of Castille and Portugal. The Novices take the duty in the same manner. Pag.10			Page 12.	

TABLE FOR THE OFFICE OF THE COMMISSIONERS OF THE POOR INFIRM WOMEN.

Rules for the Infirm Poor.	Medical Staff.	Surgeons.	Medicines.	Allowances.	Fixed. Dole of Bread.
Officers. Page 13.	Two for the town of Valletta.	Two for the town of Valletta.	To all the poor oft he four towns.	To the serious cases, one *tari* and a couple of loaves daily.	For the poor of the four towns.
Two knights of different nations, commissioners of the infirm poor of the Island.	One for the Borgo.	One for the Borgo.	Of the Island of Malta and Gozzo.	To the less serious, one *curlino* and bread daily.	*Para,* one hundred and fifty daily 150.
A clerk for the accounts of the aforesaid commissioners. Page 14.	One for the Isola.	One for the Isola.	Broth and decoctions are given, besides the usual dole.	To the disabled, two *tari* weekly, and bread daily.	Pag. 15.
Four *pitanziere* for the distribution of allowances to the four towns. Page 14. And four female assistants..	One for Burmola. Page 14.	One for Burmola. Page 14.	With the exception of women of bad character, - who must go to the House of Incurables. Page 14.	To the old women, two loaves daily. All together the amount to 150 daily. Page 16.	

Fixed Monthly Payments.	Casetta and House of Incurables..	Ecclesiastics.	Doctors and Surgeons.	Medicines.	Description of Food.
To the different disabled persons in every town, to the amount of 70 *scudi* monthly.	The Holy Religion supports the aforesaid House.	One priest subject to the Ordinary, paid by the Holy Religion.	The two medical men of the poor of the town..	Medicines oft he dispensary oft he Infirmary of every kind, authorised by the commissioners' signature.	Very good broth, pottages, and sops.
	Officers. The two commissioners of the poor.	Page 17.	The two surgeons of the same poor.		Small balls of paste (called *guicchetti*) strongly made of rice-paste.
Page 15.	One clerk for the accounts, and one for the *mancia*.		Page 17.	Page 17.	Gallinas. Pigeons. Fowls, Veal. Beef. Forcedmeat.
	A barber and dispenser of medicines. A *governatrice*. Four servants. One cross. One domestic. Page. 16.				Fricassees. Stew. Eggs. Almondpaste. Plums. Raisins. Refreshments. Biscuits. Good wine. And other restoratives. Pag. 18.

Number of Wards.	Mercurial Anointing	Fixed Charities	Annual Expenses.	Doctors and Surgeons are paid by the Common Treasury
Ward for decoctions.	Twice a year – namely, May and September.	The foundlings from the Falanga are attended to in the *Casetta*.	Without medicines.	The medicines are reckoned in the Infirmary account.
Old ward for those with fever.	No one is refused. Page 19.	Disabled old women are received.	Without reckoning the dole of bread, &c.	
Ward for the anointers.		Also poor women in child-birth, of weak mind, or shamefaced.	Without the doctors' and surgeons' salary.	
Ward for the wounded.		The overplus of soup and bread is given away to other poor coming there.	The commissioners' expense amounts every year to about 3900 *scudi*.	
Ward for the old.				
			Page 19.	_____Sc. 3900.
Page 18.		Page 19.		

Part III

THE

HISTORY

OF THE

Knights of MALTA.

By Monf. L'Abbé de Vertot.

ILLUSTRATED

With LXXI. Heads of the Grand Masters, &c. Engraved by the beſt Hands in *France*, from the Original Paintings, under the Inſpection of Monf. *Bologne*, Director of the Royal Academy of Painting. With Maps by Monf. *de Lille*, and the Plans and Fortifications of *Malta* by the Chevalier *de Tigné*. And a compleat Index to the whole.

Vol. II.

LONDON:

Printed for G. Strahan in *Cornhil*; F. Gyles over-againſt *Grey's-Inn* in *Holborn*; Meſſ. Woodman and Lyon in *Ruſſel-ſtreet*, *Covent-Garden*; D. Browne without *Temple-Bar*; Meſſ. Groenewegen, Prevost, and Vanderhoeck, in the *Strand*; C. Davis in *Pater-Noſter-Row*; and T. Osborne near *Grey's-Inn* Walks. MDCCXXVIII.

THE OLD AND NEW

STATUTES

Of the ORDER of

St. JOHN of JERUSALEM,

Tranflated from the Edition of BORGOFORTE,

A. D. M, DC, LXXVI.

By Order of the Chapter of the Great Priory of France.

Of Hospitality.

TITLE IV.

That the brothers use hospitality.

CUSTOM.

1. Hospitality is one of the most eminent acts of piety and humanity: all christian people agree in this opinion, because it comprehends all other acts. It ought to be exercised and esteemed by all good men, much more by such as are for distinguishing themselves by the name of the knights hospitallers. And for this reason, we ought not to apply our selves more particularly to any other function, than to that from which our order receives its denomination.

Of the comptrollers of the infirmary.

Br. JOHN DE LASTIC.

2. That our infirmary may be governed with the greater exactness and diligence, we decree, that two comptrollers be chose every year by the master and his council, out of different languages; who shall visit the lick carefully every day, and if they find any thing wanting that is necessary for their cure, they shall provide it immediately. The director of the infirmary shall be obliged to give them every month an account in writing of all that he has laid out: if this be not done, he by whose fault it happens shall be turned out of his office.

How the comptrollers, the secretary of the infirmary, and the commander of the little commandry, ought to conduct themselves.

Br. FABRICIO DE CARRETTO.

3. To prevent accidents which may easily happen, we enact, that the comptrollers of the infirmary, as soon as they are chosen by the master and council, shall take an oath in the council that they will well and faithfully execute their office, for the relief of the gentlemen that are sick, and will keep an exact journal of every thing that is laid out, either in the apothecary's office or in the infirmary, which is to be paid out of the common treasury. The like oath shall be taken by the secretary of the infirmary, as soon as he has been presented by the great hospitaller, according to ancient usage, to the master and his council, and been approved of by them. The commander of the little commandry shall do as much, and shall promise to give nothing to the sick, without the order of the physicians, and the knowledge of the comptrollers, who shall put it down in their accompts: for no expence that is not made in this method, shall be passed or allowed.

Br. JOHN DE LASTIC.

4. The comptrollers of the infirmary shall every evening examine the expence that has been made in the day, and shall put their names to the accompt; otherwise it must not be allowed by the procurators of the common treasury.

That an inventory be made of the goods of the infirmary.

The same MASTER.

5. We enjoin the comptrollers and the hospitaller to make strict search every year for the legacies, gifts, and goods of the infirmary, and shall take an inventory thereof in due form, which they shall sign and seal with their own seals, in the presence of the director of

the infirmary, the prior, and two witnesses: they shall insert in this inventory all vessels of gold, silver, tin and brass; all beds, blankets, sheets, tents, and every thing belonging to them, together with all furniture, and other things used for the Service of the chapel of the palace, of the chambers, kitchen, and other offices, and put down a valuation of every article. They shall also put a mark upon the goods, that they may know them again and take care that every thing be put in a safe, clean and convenient place. We likewise order the director of the infirmary to take nothing out from thence, either privately or openly, directly or indirectly, or to change or convert them to any other use.

Of visiting the apothecary's room.

The same MASTER.

6. To prevent the ill qualities of medicines doing any mischief to the sick, we order, that the apothecary's room shall be visited by the hospitaller and the comptrollers, in the presence of the physicians, as often as they shall judge proper; and the physicians shall, in their presence, examine the drugs very carefully and exactly, and see whether the shop is well furnished with them, and whether any drugs be wanting that are proper or necessary for the sick, that they may not want relief by the apothecary's fault.

Br. JAMES DE MILLY.

7. We enjoin the director of the infirmary, and the comptrollers, to have the statutes that relate to the hospital, wrote on a fair skin of parchment, which shall be fixed to a board and hung up in the palace of the sick, to be seen by all the world; that the statutes which are made for them may be the more surely and exactly observed.

Of the hospitaller's seal.

The same MASTER.

8. For the security of the goods and furniture provided for the use of the sick, we order the hospitaller or his lieutenant to have a steel seal, to mark the coverlets, furniture and other goods that will bear sealing, to prevent their being changed, carried away or embezzelled: which seal shall be put in a leathern bag, scaled with the seals of the hospitaller or his lieutenant, and of the comptrollers, and shall be kept by the director of the infirmary. The plate and other goods which are not in use every day, shall be put in a place apart, and the keys of it kept by the director and comptrollers.

That a chaplain should be deputed with the prior of the infirmary.

Br. JOHN DE LASTIC.

9. We require the hospitaller to depute some chaplain of our order of good life and conversation, whom he shall first present to the prior of the church, to be approved of and confirmed by him. The chaplain shall say four masses a week in the infirmary, and the prior three, that the sick may hear mass every day. He that officiates shall pray to God for the health of their fouls and bodies, and the usual salary shall be paid them. They shall be obliged to hear confessions, to administer the holy eucharist, to bury them after their death, and, in a word, to do everything that is necessary either for the saving of their souls, or the christian interment of their bodies.

Of the exemption of the prior of the infirmary.

Br. JAMES DE MILLY.

10. The prior of the infirmary ought to be careful and diligent in attending on the sick, especially in what concerns their salvation. We therefore order him to do his utmost in this respect, to say mass to them, to administer the holy sacraments to them, and acquit himself faithfully of every other part of his duty. And that he may do

this with the greater convenience, we exempt him from caravans, and allow him to keep a servant, for whose maintenance he shall receive out of the common treasury the same quantity of wheat that a brother knight receives.

Of the physicians of the infirmary.

Br. JOHN DE LASTIC.

11. Learned and experienced physicians shall be called in for the relief of the sick, and shall take an oath in the presence of eight brothers of the languages; that they will do their best for the recovery of the sick, following the practice and writings of the moil approved physicians; and that they will visit them at least twice a day without fail, to prescribe what is proper for them, notwithstanding any other business upon their hands. The director of the infirmary shall be by at their visits, and the secretary, who shall write down with great exactness all that the physicians prescribe. The physicians shall have a salary out of the common treasury, and may neither demand nor receive any thing from the lick for their sees.

Of the Chirurgeons.

The same MASTER.

12. We order, that for the same service of the sick they pitch upon two chirurgeons that are prudent, discreet, and skillful in their profession. They must be first examined and approved of by the physicians of the infirmary: otherwise we forbid them to be admitted.

That the director of the infirmary visits the sick every night.

The same MASTER.

13. The director of the infirmary ought to be very careful of the sick, that no accident happen by his negligence. We enjoin him therefore to go attended by a faithful servant, to visit them with

prudence and discretion at the hour of compline and day break, speak to them, exhort them, encourage them and assist them all he can. The comptrollers, when they go thither in the morning, shall enquire whether he has done his duty; if he has failed in any respect, they shall give him a severe reprimand, and order him to be more exact for the future; in failure of which, they must provide somebody else. The director of the infirmary shall take care to give the lick none but the belt and moll delicate forts of food, as pullets and chickens, good bread and good wine, to supply them with good nourishment: the comptrollers are likewise ordered to take care that the sick be so treated.

Of the modest carriage of the sick in the infirmary.

The same MASTER.

14. To restrain the insolence and immodest behaviour of some, we order the sick, as well brothers as seculars, to carry themselves with great civility and modesty in the infirmary; that nothing be given to them but what the physicians order: if they are so bold and importunate as to demand any thing else, we forbid it to be given them. Such likewise as begin to be better shall make no noise, nor play at cards, dice or chefs: they shall not read histories nor chronicles aloud, tho' they may read them to themselves, and without making any noise. Such as will not correct themselves of this ill habit shall receive nothing from the infirmary, shall be turned out of the company of the sick, and go to live elsewhere they please: they do not deserve the advice of physicians or the benefit of medicines that flight the precepts and rules of physick. The director is to take care this rule be observed, otherwise he shall be turned out of his port. The brothers may continue there for ten days after they are out of the physicians hands, and eat at the director of the infirmary's table, the expence of which shall be made good to him out of the common treasury.

Br. ALPHONSUS of PORTUGAL.

15. When the brothers fall sick they may continue for three days in their own chambers, whither every thing that they want shall be sent them from the infirmary, the same as if they were there: but if they do not go thither after that time, they shall not be assisted with any necessaries at the expence of the order.

That the brothers confess themselves, and make their disappropriation when they go into the infirmary.

Br. JOHN DE LASTIC.

16. We enjoin all the brothers that go sick into the infirmary, to confess themselves and receive the holy eucharist within twenty four hours afterwards. They shall likewise make their disappropriation or declaration of all their effects, which shall be sealed with the prior of the infirmary's seal. If they refuse doing it in the said space of time, they shall be expelled the infirmary, and receive no assistance thence. We enjoin likewise the director of the infirmary to keep a sufficient number of regular and diligent servants to attend on the sick, and two women of good reputation to breed up children that are found exposed, whom they must take care to have baptized.

Br. CLAUDE DE LA SENGLE.

17. All the disappropriations of our brothers that die either in the convent or elsewhere, shall be registred in the court of exchequer.

Of the wills that are to be made by secular persons sick in the infirmary.

Br. JAMES DE MILLY.

18. We order all secular persons, that are sick and received into our infirmary, to confess themselves and receive the communion; after which the prior and the comptrollers shall admonish them to make

their wills. This will shall be made by the prior, or by the secretary of the infirmary in his presence, or in the prior's absence by a priest, in the presence of two or three witnesses; and can't be annulled or broken afterwards without incurring the penalties of the canon law. The prior and secretary shall have as much authority to make it, in the presence of at least two witnesses, as two publick notaries would have. It shall be registered in a book, for the security of the rights of such as are intitled to the estate or effects of the deceased. If the secular persons that are sick, are not in a condition, or do not care to make their will, the director of the infirmary and the comptrollers shall order the prior or secretary to make an inventory of all that belongs to them, in the presence of two witnesses, to restore it to them if they recover their health, and to deliver it to their heirs if they chance to die: and the effects recited in the inventory are locked up in a safe place under the keys of the director and the comptrollers.

Br. CLAUDE DE LA SENGLE.
19. The comptrollers are ordered to see that the wills of seculars that die in our infirmary be executed punctually.

The manner of burying deceased brothers.

Br. NICOLAS DE LORGUE.
20. Tis a very decent practice in the funeral honours paid to our brothers, that their bodies should be covered with the habit given them at their entrance into the order, and which they wore afterwards all their life; and therefore we order that all the brothers of the hospital, when it pleases God to call them, shall be buried in their mantles à bec, i. e. with points, and the white cross.

That the corps of seculars deceased be buried handsomely.

Br. JOHN DE LASTIC.

21. We order that the corps of secular persons that die in our infirmary should be buried handsomely; that the chaplains shall walk before the corps and pray for the foul of the deceased: that the four persons that carry the bier shall wear black robes, which shall be made and kept for this particular purpose: the director of the infirmary is to see that this be done.

That no body shall appear in mourning at the death of our brothers.

Br. CLAUDE DE LA SENGLE.

22. We order that the corps of our brothers shall be buried honourably: we expressly forbid all persons, as well our brothers as seculars, to appear in mourning at the funeral of a brother, or even of the grand master himself, in what place forever he should die.

Of the opening of the coffers of the deceased.

Br. JAMES DE MILLY.

23. To prevent any embezzelling the effects of the deceased, we expressly forbid all persons to open the coffers of such as die in the infirmary, but in the presence of the hospitaller, the director of the infirmary, and the two comptrollers. If they find any goods therein that may be of service in the infirmary, they shall not be applied to any other use.

Of the four hundred florins left to the infirmary by Villeragut.

Br. CLAUDE DE LA SENGLE.

24. As it is very reasonable to comply with the lift will and intention of testators, we allow none of our brothers, what authority for-

ever he is invested with, to dispose of the sum of florins that was left as a legacy to our infirmary by brother James de Villeragut castellan of Emposta, or of any improvement that has either been made already, or shall hereafter be made of it: unless it be the great conservator of our convent, who may dispose of it for the service of the sick according to the will and intent of the testator.

Of the privilege of the infirmary.

Br. FABRICIO DEL CARETTO.

25. We enact, that if any criminal comes to take sanctuary in our infirmary, and any doubt be made whether he shall have the benefit of it or no, the hospitaller, or his lieutenant, shall, at the instance of the castellan or judge, give order for his safe keeping in the infirmary, till the case has been fully examined into: and if it appears that he ought to enjoy the privilege of sanctuary, he shall be sent out of the island on the first ship that sails, as has been the ancient practice.

The cases in which the infirmary cannot serve for a sanctuary.

Br. CLAUDE DE LA SENGLE.

26. The privilege of the infirmary shall be of no use to assassines, to such as pillage the country by night, to incendiaries, to sodomites, to conspirators, nor to robbers, such likewise as are guilty of murdering any body by ambuscado, wilfully in cold blood, treacherously, or by poison; the servants too of our brothers, such as have attempted the lives of our brothers, judges, or ministers of justice, persons that are in debt, such as have committed crimes within the infirmary it self, or designedly in hopes of finding sanctuary there, false witnesses, sacrilegious persons, robbers on the high way; all these are excluded from the privilege of it.

The same MASTER.
27. We order that they shall continue to distribute the alms that used to be given in our commandries.

ORDINANCES.

Of the general chapter held A. D. 1631. by the most eminent and most reverend Grand Master,

Br. ANTHONY DE PAULE.
In the name of the most holy and undivided trinity, father, son and holy ghost Amen. The sixteen most reverend capitulary lords, chosen by the eminent and most reverend lord brother Anthony de Paule grand master, and the sacred general chapter on Wednesday May 14, 1631. the third day of the chapter being no holy day, and deputed commissaries to consult, decree, and ordain every thing that may promote the honour and service of the sacred order and knights of the hospital of St. John of Jerusalem, being retired the same day into the usual conclave, in presence of the most illustrious lord Louis Seristorio, inquisitor general in this island, deputed by our holy father pope Urban VIII. and the holy apostolic see, and presiding there, for the observation of his holines's brief, which was there read and published the same day, after taking the oath and receiving the charge of the most eminent and most reverend lord grand master, having their own duty, and the tenour of the statutes before their eyes, void of all passion and interest, and looking up to our lord Jesus Christ suffering and dying for us, they have continued their session from the said third day to the twentieth capitulary day, being no festival; and the most illustrious lord president having then, at the desire of his eminence, prolonged the chapter by his apostolical authority, the said sixteen lords meeting again on the seventh of the present month of June, at the found of the bell, as usual, at the motion of the venerable lord brother, Toussaints de

Terves Boisgirant, hospitaller, as the principal person of their number, being all united in brotherly love, after seriously weighing and debating every particular point referred to them, and making use of balloting wherever it was necessary, have ordained, constituted and decreed as follows.

OF HOSPITALITY.

TITLE IV

The same sixteen reverend lords, resolving to revive the form of oath which the comptrollers of the infirmary used to take formerly before the master, immediately after their election, have ordained, that it shall be taken in the following manner, and shall be wrote on a table and fixed up in the infirmary to be seen by all the world.

Form of the oath of the comptrollers of the holy infirmary.

1. N. Comptroller of the holy infirmary, make a solemn oath to God to use the utmost care in visiting, relieving and providing all proper sustenance for the sick that are kept in the infirmary; that I will be careful to reform all neglects that I can discover, to examine every day the expences that are there made, to sign with my own hand all such as appear to me to be reasonable, to accompt every month with the director of the infirmary for all that he has laid out and provided for the sick, to draw up every day an exact account of all the remedies ordered by the physicians out of the apothecary's shop, which shall come to my knowledge, and to sign it with my own hand, to charge nothing else to the accompt of the treasury, and to discharge all the duties of my office with all manner of charity and exactness, according to the statutes, and ordinances, and laudable customs of the order. So help me God, and his holy gospel.

The same lords, after examining the statutes made by the venerable council on June 1, 1629 for the good government of the infirmary, have resolved, in way of ballot, to approve and confirm them, and have ordained that they shall be executed, as if they were statutes of the general chapter, and for that purpose have inserted them in this place, as follows.

2. That the incurables shall not be put any longer in a distinct place from the infirmary, but such place shall be suppressed, as also the little house appointed some years ago, for the receiving of sick women, because the order is obliged to maintain the holy exercise of hospitality in the hospital of the holy infirmary, but not to multiply the places designed for such use, nor to load the treasury with salaries, pittances, and other things granted to the officers that take care of them.

3. That the treasury shall furnish no remedies or other necessaries to any sick but such as are actually in the infirmary, and not to such as would be taken care of in their chambers, who shall be obliged to pay for every thing that is taken up for them in the apothecary's shop by the physician's prescription: Enjoining the comptrollers to give in, every six months, to the court of exchequer an account of every thing that has been taken up by any of them: The several articles whereof shall be taxed by the first physician, according to which the venerable procurators of the treasury shall regulate the sums due from every one. In cafe however the brother's distemper be of such a nature, that he ought not, according to the physician's opinion, be admitted into the infirmary, his eminence the grand master shall order what is proper to be done in such case, by the advice of the venerable hospitaller, or his lieutenant.

4. That no pittances nor medicines shall be given out of the infirmary, unless it be to poor women, upon the prescriptions of physicians that have salaries out of the treasury, or from the people,

signed by one of the commissaries deputed to visit the poor sick, that the hospital of the infirmary may be always free and open to receive sick persons, as well subjects of the orders, as others that shall repair thither to be cured of their diseases, according to its ancient and laudable custom.

5. That notwithstanding the ordinance above, they shall not fail to continue the charity they have hitherto used in furnishing remedies gratis to the monasteries of St. Ursula, the penitent sisters of the city Valette, and the capucins.

6. That sides the register of wills and testaments and disappropriations, the secretary of the infirmary shall keep, upon a little table in the hall, a great book, in which he shall write down exactly the name, surname and countrey of every sick person, the day and hour that he came in and was sent back, on that he died, charging it home on the conscience of the venerable hospitaller or his lieutenant, to take care that this article be punctually executed, as of great importance for the government of the infirmary, on pain against the secretary of being turned out of his office.

7. That notwithstanding the statute of the precedent general chapter, there shall be only two comptrollers, to do their duty and take care of the sick in the infirmary according to our statutes: The venerable council shall depute however two other officers with the title of commissary visitors, to examine how the sick poor are treated, who shall be supplied with food and remedies according to the prescription of the physicians, who shall be obliged to set down the names and surnames of the sick, and the places of their abode, that they may afterwards be signed by one of the commissaries, without which the comptrollers shall take no notice of it.

8. That the physicians and surgeons shall set down in the book of the prescriptions of the infirmary, (as they do in those which they

give for abroad) the day, month and year, with the quality and quantity of the drugs and medicines all at length, without making use of abbreviations or cyphers, forbidding them to write any thing down in this book for any other persons but such as are actually sick in the infirmary.

9. That the two practising physicians and surgeons, that have stipends, shall lye every night, without fail, in the infirmary.

10. That they take very particular care to oblige the sick, as soon as they have been taken in, to dispose themselves to receive the sacraments of penance and the eucharist, especially if they are our brothers, according to the sixteenth article of this title, which we charge expressly on the conscience of the prior and vice-prior of the infirmary.

11. That this last post be always given to a Maltese, because the greatest part of the sick are vassals to the order, but still without hurting the prerogative of the venerable hospitaller.

12. That they observe inviolably the fifth and eighth articles of this title, where mention is made of the effects and goods of the infirmary, of the inventory that ought to be taken of them, and the marks that should be put upon them to prevent their being either changed or fold.

13. That the comptrollers, among other branches of their care, take the pains sometimes to examine whether they actually give the sick the remedies that are prescribed by the physicians and entered into the book.

14. They have suppressed the abuse that was introduced of the comptrollers assuming an authority to distribute, at the expence of the common treasury, the pittance and other things of the infirmary, without the prescription of the physicians, or the directions of the

superiors, under pretence of extraordinaries: They shall have no power to dispose of any thing, particularly of bread, which they do as they please, under pretence of giving it in charity, but it shall be disposed of by the commissaries appointed for that purpose, so that the duties of the two offices be not confounded; theirs relates only to the sick; the others business is to relieve the poor.

15. Acccording to the order of the venerable council of September 18, 1579, they have ordained, as well for the convenience of the sick as the ease of the treasury, that the apothecary's room in the infirmary shall be, for the future, supplied, as formerly, by the druggists, and not by the officers of the treasury; and this by the orders of the venerable procurators who shall advance the money, and do all they can to help the druggists in the purchase and providing of the necessary drugs and medicines at the proper time, referring it to their prudence to make a bargain for them upon the estimates which shall be given them by the druggists.

16. The physicians may, for the convenience of the secular officers that the order gives salaries to, who shall be sick at home, to prescribe them remedies from the infirmary, which shall be discounted to them, according to the regulation of the venerable procurators of the common treasury.

17. That they restore the good order for keeping of the cloaths of such as shall be sick in the infirmary, which shall be locked up in coffers, though it were only to prevent their going out before they are quite cured, and committing other indiscretions,

18. That they do not receive any secular into the infirmary, not even the servants of the knights, under pretence of taking physick by way of precaution, as several do, especially in the spring, which is a great charge to the order, whose institution is only to relieve such as are actually sick in the infirmary.

19. That the venerable procurators of the treasury give the comptrollers instructions in order to receive the accompts of the director of the infirmary, more particular than what they give at present, which is too confused and perplexed.

20. For the having always a perfect knowledge of all the goods and utensils of the infirmary, that have been given by the executors of such foundations as have been made for the service of the sick, they have ordered the secretary to keep a distinct register, in which there shall be entered, under the several distinct titles of each foundation, the quality of the goods that have been received, with the date of their reception, and the name of the person that delivered them, which reception shall be signed by the comptrollers in the register itself.

21. That all pittances given out of the infirmary to poor women that are sick, shall, for the future, be given in money, and not in victuals.

22. The same lords, after a scrutiny in the way of ballot, have ordained, that the statute of the grand master Verdale, which is the twenty third of the title of baillis, and relates to the choice of the director of the infirmary, shall be observed according to its form and tenour, and that officer shall be always chose out of the brother knights.

23. The same lords, considering that all our brothers were particularly obliged to use hospitality, and to attend the sick themselves, and that if our brothers of the venerable languages went thither all at a time, it would occasion a great deal of confusion, and there being no regulation ever made as yet in this point, have ordained, that from and after the Sunday immediately following the publication of the present general chapter, as it belongs to the venerable language of Provence to begin, the venerable great commander, or

his lieutenant, shall send to the infirmary to wait upon the sick, as many brother knights, servants of arms, or novices, as he shall think necessary, to the number of seven at least, who shall attend there all the week, morning and evening. Such as shall neglect to do so, after being named by their pilier, shall be punished with the septaine.

24. That the venerable hospitaller and great conservator shall, every fix months, visit the goods of the infirmary in the prefence of the comptrollers, on pain of being deprived of their deliberative voice in the venerable councils, till they have effectually executed the present statute.

25. That besides the ordinary visitations, the grand master and the venerable council shall depute, every three months, two commissaries of the said council, of the most considerable and intelligent members of it, who, for the better direction of the infirmary and relief of the sick, shall visit the infirmary along with the venerable hospitaller, and inform themselves exactly of every thing that can either contribute or be prejudicial to it, and, upon their report, the grand master and council shall make such regulations as they shall see fit and are proper for the good management of the infirmary, and for the relief of the poor, though it should be necessary for that end to change, or even abolish entirely, any of the chapter ordinances that relate to it, and make new ones.

26. That the director of the infirmary shall give the comptrollers a just and true account of the wine that is pent there every day, to correct the abuses which are introduced in that particular to the detriment of the common treasury: They shall pass it in his accompts, as well as the fowl, pullets, eggs, and other provisions, at the rate that they are generally fold at the market, notwithstanding the custom and ordinary tax which may prove sometimes to his prejudice. Enjoining the comptrollers to take care that the provi-

sions be good of their fort, and proper for the relief and recovery of the sick; that they be furnished with charity and liberality, and nothing be neglected that can be serviceable either to the soul or body, as we are engaged to do by our profession.

27. Considering the variety of languages spoke by such as are in the infirmary, the same lords have ordained, that the prior and vice-prior understand several tongues, that the sick may confess to them more easily; but this regulation shall not intrench on the right of presenting them which belongs to the venerable hospitaller and his lieutenant, according to the statutes.

28. That for two years of actual service done by the vice-prior of the infirmary in it, he shall be deemed to have made a caravan, and it shall be reckoned to him as such, all the same as if he had made it on board the gallies of the order; requiring the venerable assembly of the chaplains to allow it him without any dispute.

29. They have referred it to the venerable officers of the treasury, to find out some expedient to prevent frauds being committed in the accompts which are given to the comptrollers, of the distributions of remedies, and other drugs and medicines, when the apothecary reads them over.

30. That the physician, who is to begin his month of service, visit the sick three days before, along with the physician that is to end his; that he may not put another in his place to visit the sick, when he does not come in person, or is not hindered by some accident that can justly excuse him, on pain of paying fix tarins for every default.

31. That all the physicians and surgeons shall be obliged to assemble once a week in the infirmary, to consult about the condition of

the sick and wounded. Such as fail to be there, shall forfeit five crowns, which shall be deducted out of their salaries.

32. That they shall take but a tarin (or gigliat) a day for visiting such brothers as are sick in their chambers, on pain of losing a month of their salary: That they shall be obliged to visit the convents of the nuns of St. Ursula, of the penitents of the city of la Valette and the capucins gratis, for the month succeeding that of their service in the infirmary, as often as they are sent for, in which they shall be relieved by others in their turn as they come out of the infirmary, so that they shall be employed there and in visits abroad alternately.

33. That the two physicians who are not in their month of service, shall make each of them their visits by the week, or at least on different days, to the prison of the slaves.

34. Whereas a great quantity of remedies are distributed to poor sick people out of the infirmary, one of the physicians and surgeons, who are not actually employed in visiting the sick, shall not fail to make them at least one visit a day gratis; which they shall do either by the month or the week, as is most for their convenience. We order the venerable hospitaller, or his lieutenant, to look after the execution of the present statute.

35. That they shall keep in the infirmary, at the charge of the treasury, a man well versed in the practice of physick, who, after being duly examined by the physicians, and presented to the grand master by the venerable hospitaller, shall furnish drugs, medicines, and other necessaries for the sick at proper times, according to the prescriptions of the physicians, to whom he shall be obliged to give an exact account of the condition of the sick, that they may be able to prevent accidents, and prescribe nothing but what is proper for them.

36. That he shall be obliged to be at the infirmary when the physicians make their visits there, and to observe, with the secretary, what it is that they prescribe to be given them to eat, in order to eat, in order to follow their prescriptions.

37. That the surgeons, who have stipends, shall be obliged to visit the wounded that are in the infirmary, as often as there is occasion, in failure whereof the venerable hospitaller shall punish them as he sees fit.

38. That to prevent accidents which may happen to them, and give them speedy relief, there shall be always at least one surgeon in the infirmary, who shall keep his residence there.

39. That they shall continue to give alms to the poor Rhodians, Malteze, and others; to the orphans and widows of such as have lost their husbands and fathers in the service of the order, making however a distinction in favour of reputable and virtuous persons.

40. They have since moderated the foregoing statute, and ordained that the alms, which use to be given to various persons by the name of Rhodians out of the convent, as at Syracuse, Messina, and other places, shall cease, in proportion as they come to dye, without being continued to their successours, as has been practiced before, revoking all the graces of reservation made or to be made by the present chapter, contrary to this statute.

41. That the common treasury shall furnish every year fifty crowns of twelve tarins a piece, for the expence of the lord's supper on Maundy Thursday in passion week.

IUS VIVENS
Quellentexte zur Rechtsgeschichte
hrsg. von Prof. Dr. Heinz Holzhauer (Münster), Dr. Wolf-Dieter Barz (Karlsruhe), Prof. Dr. Andreas Roth (Mainz) und Prof. Dr. Stefan Chr. Saar (Potsdam)

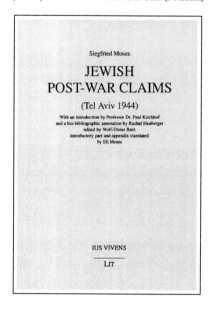

Siegfried Moses
Jewish Post-War Claims (Tel Aviv 1944)
With an introduction by Professor Dr. Paul Kirchhof and a bio-bibliographic annotation by Rachel Heuberger. Edited by Wolf-Dieter Barz. Introductory part and appendix translated by Eli Moses
It has been only recently that the long drawn out international negotiations conducted in the U.S. on the subject of the finalization of reparations to be paid by Germany to the, mainly Jewish, forced laborers of the National Socialist regime were concluded. The American-Jewish aspect of the broader subject of involvement with the aftermath of the Holocaust has already evoked an echo of wide-ranging discussions in the recently published works of Wolf Calebow, Peter Novick and Norman Finkelstein.
Bd. 6, 2001, 184 S., 35,90 €, br., ISBN 3-8258-5024-2

LIT Verlag Berlin – Münster – Wien – Zürich – London
Auslieferung Deutschland / Österreich / Schweiz: siehe Impressumsseite